MEDITATION MOMENTS to MELT the HEART

*Everyday Moments
Eternal Truths*

Fifty-two Biblical and Photographic Devotionals
To Bring Joy as You Journey through the Year

JOYCE CANARY ROSE

xulon
PRESS

Copyright © 2015 by Joyce Canary Rose

MEDITATION MOMENTS TO MELT THE HEART
Everyday Moments Eternal Truths
by Joyce Canary Rose

Harry Bollback Illustration used by permission

Printed in the United States of America.

ISBN 9781498441131

All rights reserved solely by the author. The author guarantees all contents are original and do not infringe upon the legal rights of any other person or work. No part of this book may be reproduced in any form without the permission of the author. The views expressed in this book are not necessarily those of the publisher.

Unless otherwise indicated, Scripture quotations taken from the New American Standard Bible (NASB). Copyright © 1960, 1962, 1963, 1968, 1971, 1972, 1973, 1975, 1977, 1995 by The Lockman Foundation. Used by permission. All rights reserved.

Scripture quotations taken from the King James Version (KJV)–*public domain.*

Scripture quotations taken from the New King James Version (NKJV). Copyright © 1982 by Thomas Nelson, Inc. Used by permission. All rights reserved.

Scripture quotations taken from the Holy Bible, New International Version (NIV). Copyright © 1973, 1978, 1984, 2011 by Biblica, Inc.™. Used by permission. All rights reserved.

"His Name Is Wonderful"
Audrey Mae Mieir
© Copyright 1959, Renewed 1987. Manna Music, Inc. /ASCAP (admin. By ClearBox Rights). All rights reserved.
Used by permission.

Anne Graham Lotz Quote:
Copyright © 2014 Anne Graham Lotz (AnGeL Ministries) Raleigh, North Carolina, USA.
Used by permission. All rights reservedwww.annegrahamlotz.org

"What is a Grandmother?" quote
Taken from "What Wives Wish Their Husbands Knew About Women" by James Dobson.
Copyright © 1975, 2003 by Tyndale House Publishers.
Used by permission of Tyndale House Publishers, Inc. All rights reserved.

CAT'S IN THE CRADLE
Words and Music by HARRY CHAPIN and SANDY CHAPIN
Copyright © 1974 (Renewed) STORY SONGS, LTD.
All Rights Administered by WB MUSIC CORP.
All Rights Reserved
Used By Permission of ALFRED MUSIC

www.xulonpress.com

TABLE OF CONTENTS

Confidence to Melt the Discouraged Heart xiii

Contentment to Melt the Dissatisfied Heart 37

Clarity to Melt the Doubting Heart. 57

Comfort to Melt the Despairing Heart 85

Constancy to Melt the Dedicated Heart 99

Christmas Keepsakes to Melt the Devoted Heart. 127

INTRODUCTION

Can God's faithfulness be seen on the frosting covered face of a baby celebrating his first birthday? Can harvesting blueberries teach me how to overcome fear? Can patience be heard in the laughter of a toddler?

YES! YES! YES! Lessons retrieved from God's Word can be melted into the heart through absorbing ordinary moments! The eyes of the soul can perceive Truth by looking into the eyes of a child, or by observing cloud cover after a winter snow storm. The ears of the heart can hear God's shout through the soft sweet voice of a grinning toddler! The skin of the soul can be touched by the fingers of a child! When that child reaches out and grasps her Mommy's hand, that mother can feel the presence of a holy God! And, by sharing a child's chocolate birthday cake, with blue whipped frosting, I can taste and see that God is good!

In *MEDITATION MOMENTS TO MELT THE HEART*, three points are used as a triad to lead the reader to apply God's Truth. At one point of this triangle is a touching and true story to which anyone with a love of children or nature can relate. At the second point is a candid and timeless photo which illustrates the story and adds a visual experience to the emotional one. At the top point is the trusted Word of God. An honest and life altering application of a Bible passage is given in each devotional. Encouragement for the soul is the inevitable result!

The fifty two devotionals in *MEDITATION MOMENTS TO MELT THE HEART* can be used as catalysts for weekly Bible studies. They are divided into six chapters. Each separate chapter focuses on giving hope for a different heart need. Whether disappointed or distracted, or overwhelmed by a myriad of troubles, the soul will discover answers.

If the old adage that "a picture is worth a thousand words" is true, then what must be the inestimable value of a picture *AND* a thousand words, especially when those words contain the very Word of God? *MEDITATION MOMENTS TO MELT THE HEART* is a devotional book to be assimilated into the very spiritual core of the reader. It will melt away discouragement and doubt, and fill the reader with confidence and contentment.

DEDICATION

This book is dedicated to

Our grandchildren,

Who melt my heart with everyday moments

That turn my thoughts to eternal truths.

AND

To my Lord and Savior, Jesus Christ,

I dedicate, anew,

My moments… my days… my years… my life.

My heart belongs to You.

ACKNOWLEDGEMENTS

To my husband, Alan, and our daughters, Tabitha, Rebecca, Sarah, and Bethany, as well as all my family and friends who encouraged me to compile these devotionals into a book…thank you.

To Wendy, whose teaching and skills in photography, taught me how to look beyond the obvious, see the nuances of God's creation, and compose them into an image that can tell a story…thank you.

To Pastor and Mrs. Wilson, who have been our mentors and spiritual parents, guiding us through the joys and storms of life with sound Biblical counsel…thank you.

To Sarah, who read and advised and edited…thank you.

To Shirley, whose mentorship and friendship God used to lay a Scriptural foundation that taught me the priority and ministry of family…thank you. And…thank you for your gracious endorsement.

Above all…to my Lord and Savior Jesus Christ…THANK YOU.

"Let the words of my mouth and the meditation of my heart
Be acceptable in Your sight,
O Lord, my rock and my Redeemer." (Psalm 19:14)

ENDORSEMENT

Seldom does a person have the opportunity to see the life-time growth and development of another person, other than their own children. I remember Joyce Rose as a young mother, married to a man who was a pastor of a country church, and working to support his family in a new business. This is a formula for stress and difficulty in the best of situations.

Joyce came to me, knowing that I had gone through similar stress in my own life. Actually, I was just ahead of her by a few years. There was a great deal to learn in our days of being young mothers married to "men in ministry".

Flash forward to when her youngest child, a beautiful young lady named Bethany, came to the Word of Life Bible Institute. Her mother suggested, if they still had staff members assigned to the students, to ask for me…saying we knew each other and I was easy to talk to…another opportunity that was very unusual and an absolute delight. I grew to know and love the daughter, just as I had known and loved her Mom.

Joyce has written these words from a heart of love for the Savior, His Word, her husband, her children, and now, her beautiful grandchildren. She is at ease with her words, and conveys what she has learned in a comfortable, endearing way ... (but then, I AM prejudiced!). I enjoyed the privilege of reading it early on, and know you will enjoy the concepts from Scripture, the applications to life and living, and her use of word pictures (as well as REAL photos).

Take the time to enjoy these pages. I know you will be drawn to the message of Christ in everyday moments, in everyday language, and in everyday situations. Be sure you share what YOU have learned along your journey, just as JOYCE ROSE has done.

Mrs. Shirley Bubar,
Mentor of women enrolled in Word of Life Bible Institute
And teacher of "Christian Womanhood", for twenty years

*CONFIDENCE
TO MELT THE
DISCOURAGED HEART*

"PEEK-A-BOO"

"Peek-a-boo"
That is what this picture says to me.
Oh, I know that Addison is too young to be thinking about that game.
But...isn't this photo the best??
Don't you want to pick her up and squeeze her?
My heart just melts.
I want to "freeze frame" this moment.
I want to super glue this snapshot to the wall of my heart!
I want to *KEEP* it!

I believe that God gives us such moments as gifts.
James 1:17 says that *"Every good thing given and every perfect gift is from above..."*
At times, God likes to "surprise" us with "peek-a-boo moments".
Such moments may be unexpected,
But they are to keep and treasure and ponder!

Jesus' mother, Mary, had such moments.
What did she do with them?
Luke 2 tells us that, after the visit of the shepherds,
"...Mary treasured all these things, pondering them in her heart."
Again, when the Child was 12 years old,
Mary and Joseph could not find Him for three days.
Finally, they located him in the temple.
His response?
"...Did you not know that I had to be in my Father's house?"
"And He went down with them and came to Nazareth,
And He continued in subjection to them..."
Mary's response?
"And His mother treasured all these things in her heart."

Treasure those moments!
The unexpected surprise gifts God gives to you.
Take "snapshots" and hold them in your heart.
Be thankful and think about them!
Hold on to them!

As I was contemplating this "peek-a-boo" meditation moment,
I opened my *Daily Bread* to see the title "Boo".
I read it, and then sat on my couch praying and pondering.
What would you have me say, Lord?

As I gazed out my window, I was "surprised"!
Surprised by another "peek-a-boo moment".
A deer was peeking at me through the slats of our deck railing.
I was just amazed at God's individual and loving attention.

Coincidence, you say?

No!
It was one of God's surprise gifts!
It was as if He was saying,
"Peek-a-boo. I see you!"
And then, the question,
"Do you see *ME*?"

Do I see *HIM*?
That is the question!
HE is everywhere! He shouts His glory into my ears!
He magnifies Himself in my vision!
His fragrance fills my life.
I taste...and I see that the Lord is good!
He touches my life...and I have peace!

And...If I pay attention...
I see the "peek-a-boo; I see you" moments.
He surprises me with unexpected gifts!
Gifts I am to treasure and keep and ponder.

Gifts...like a verse from the Bible filling my mind...
At the very moment I need God's guidance.
Gifts...like an incredible answer to prayer.
Gifts...like a call from a grandchild just when I need a smile.
Gifts...like one of His creation peeking through the deck rails.
Gifts...like the smile, and grin, and yawn, and frown,
And snuggles and "peek-a-boo" poses...
From our newborn granddaughter!

Pay Attention!
Don't miss them!
Hang on to those moments!
Treasure them and hold them in your heart!
They come from your loving Heavenly Father!

"REFLECTIONS"

Hmmmm...
I wonder...
What is on Nathan's mind?
Is he looking at his own reflection?
Is he peering at the brick wall?
Is he looking beyond all that?

How often do I ponder...reflect...consider?
When I do...do I just look at myself?
Do I focus on what appears to be a brick wall facing me?
Or...am I able to look beyond that wall?

Psalm 77 is a psalm of a troubled believer.
His soul *"refused to be comforted"*.
His spirit *"grows faint"*.
He then considers *"the years of long ago"*.
He meditates...his spirit ponders.
He wonders, *"Has God forgotten to be gracious…?"*

Have you ever wondered, "Where is God?"
"Why do my prayers appear to go unanswered?"
When I am overwhelmed and discouraged,
Do I become self-absorbed?
Do I see only the brick wall blocking my answer?
Or am I able to change my perspective and look beyond?

In spite of his anguish,
The psalmist chose to change his perspective.
He chose to focus on what He knew was true.
He chose to remember what God had already done.
He says, *"Surely, I will remember Your wonders of old.*
I will meditate on all Your work, and muse on Your deeds."

God is ALWAYS at work...
He is forever faithful.

I trusted Christ as Savior when I was in my teens.
For years, I prayed for my grandpa to be saved.
I loved my grandpa, but he had a hard life.
Cursing was part of his regular vocabulary.
I prayed... "Nothing" happened.

When I was in my mid 20's, I received a phone call.
My grandfather was in the hospital.
I knew I had to go see him.
I knew I had to give him the gospel.
My husband and I went.
After we talked, Grandpa looked at me.
He said some words I have never forgotten.
Grandpa said:
"When I was a teen-ager, my pastor said to me,
'Jimmy, don't wait until you are on your deathbed to get saved.'
Well, here I am."
That evening, my grandfather got saved!

Why do I tell you this story?
I tell you because I wonder...
How many times did that pastor give the gospel?
How many prayers did that pastor say for my grandpa?
How discouraged did he get?
How often did he wonder if this boy would ever believe?

I do know one thing.
That pastor died before that prayer was answered...
BUT it was answered!
Praise the Lord!
God is faithful throughout all generations.
God is always at work.

So...when I get discouraged...
When my prayers *SEEM* to go unanswered...
When I wonder if a loved one will ever get saved...
When I pray and circumstances remain the same...
I reflect... and I remember...
"You are the God who works wonders."
You are the God who answers prayer!
You are the God who is not bound by time!
"Great is Thy Faithfulness!"

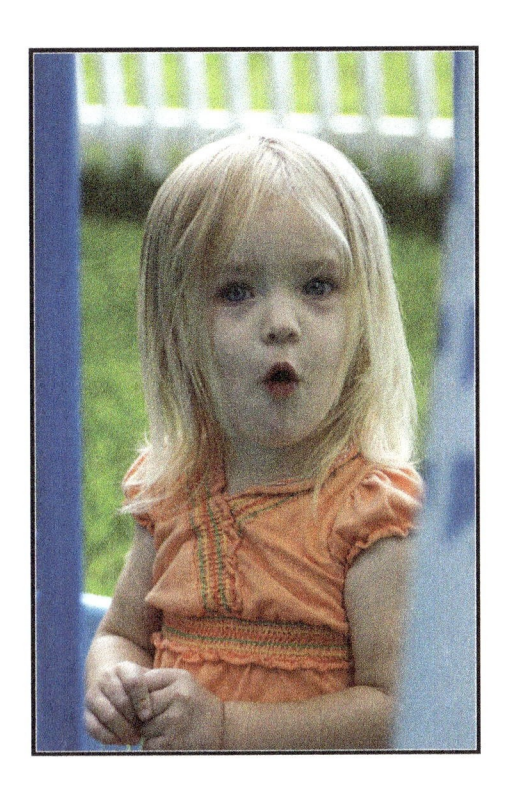

"NO More Cheese"

Caroline is a beautiful model.
Grandma loves to capture images of special moments with her.
But ...sometimes Grandma can get carried away...
I mean, enough is enough!
And Caroline will let me know.
If she wants her photo taken, she will flash a beautiful smile and say, "cheeeese".
But if she has had enough of picture taking,
She will look at me and say, "Gramma...no more cheese!"
And so...I put my camera away (usually).

But...sometimes, Grandma does NOT put away the camera.
After all...I am the adult....right?
Sometimes, I think a better image is coming…
So...I wait, camera in hand.
And often...a better image *DOES* come.
After all, I would have missed the image below if I had stopped too soon.
I would have missed the moment when Caroline was enjoying her swing...
Smile on her face; hair flowing wildly in the breeze!

Meditation Moments To Melt The Heart

"Wheeee...this is fun, Gramma!"

I love Caroline!
I would do just about anything to keep her happy!
But...sometimes...good things don't happen as soon as she would like.
Sometimes...she has to wait!!

Isn't a similar thing true of our relationship with God?
Jesus loves us!
He says," *I came that they might have life, and have it abundantly." (John 10:10)*
God wants us to have an abundant life.
But things don't always happen in *OUR* time frame...
Because our Heavenly Father is looking for a better "image"!

What kind of image is God "waiting for"?
Romans 8:29 tells us...
"For those whom He foreknew" (that's us) *"... He also predestined
To become conformed to the image of HIS SON…"*

WOW! God actually wants me to look like Jesus...
To talk like Jesus...
To walk like Jesus...
To be like Jesus...
Conformed to the image of Jesus!

God's plan is the "big picture"!
When I am walking through a valley...
And I am tired...
And I want to exclaim, *"NO MORE"*,
I take His hand, and He walks with me...
And He teaches me how to take the hands of others...
And walk with them through their valleys.

When I am discouraged with myself and my failures,
And I am tempted to say, *"NO MORE*...I give up!"
I go to Him...and He strengthens me...

And He gives me empathy for others.

When I can't understand my trying circumstances,
And I want to say..."*NO MORE*",
He teaches me to rest in Him.
He shows me that, when I can't see His hand...
I can still trust His heart...
And I learn to share His love with others.

So...on those days when I am totally frustrated...
During those times when the trials have gone on too long...
When my heart is hurting...
When the moments of despair have dragged on into hours...or days...or months,
When the abundant life seems out of reach for a while,
When I just want to cry out to God and say,
"NO MORE!"...
I remember the "big picture"!

I may want to give up on myself!
But God will never give up on me!
He will complete His work.
I can trust Him!

And so...resting in *HIM*, I continue on...
Comforted by *HIS* presence.
Consoled by *HIS* greater purpose.
Confident of *HIS* promises.
Content to know *HE* has a plan.

I realize that I tend to look at circumstances through my zoom lens.
I narrow in, observing things from my own limited perspective.
But God?
God alone is truly able to use the wide lens of eternity!
And *HE* holds the camera!!!
HE WILL NOT GIVE UP!!
He is teaching me and preparing me to be used to help others while I am here,
And to finally fully be like Him in eternity.

HE will not be finished until...
When He "takes my picture"...
I reflect Jesus!

Someday...
Finally...
When I am with *HIM*...
When I see *HIM* "face to face",
The image will be "perfect".
I will be conformed to the image of *HIS SON!!*
I will be like Jesus!

"THE DOTTED LINE"

I nestle my face into her fine silky hair.
I slowly breathe in the soft scent of baby lotion.
My hand rests on her back as it gently rises and falls.
I hear her soft breathing…baby breaths.
I am still.
I am holding on to the moment…the dot of this second.
My face lightly brushes against her soft petal skin.
I look into her gentle face…trying to take a mental photo to keep.
All the time, knowing that I will never really have this exact second again.
Knowing that every dot on the timeline of life…hers, and mine, is different.
Knowing that changes come slowly…but they come.
Life is bittersweet.

I think back!
The subtle scent of Addy's hair reminds me.
Her Mommy.
I nestled my face into her hair, too.
I breathed in her baby scent.
I rested my hand on her back as it gently rose and fell with each breath.
I heard her soft breathing…baby breaths.
I was still.
I tried holding onto the moment…but it slipped away.
I felt her soft petal skin against my face.
I looked into her gentle face…took many photos.
But each second was different.
Every dot on her timeline represented a change.
Some changes I welcomed. Others I fought. To no avail.

Bittersweet.

I think back farther.
Do I dare?
My own grandma…decades ago!
She nestled her face into my hair.
When she was close, I breathed in her earthy fragrance,
The sweet and salty fragrance of a gardener.
I rested my hand in hers, and shared her life.
I wanted to hold onto those moments, too.
I felt her soft wilting petal skin.
I looked into her wrinkled gentle face.
But…again…every dot on her timeline represented change.
Few changes I welcomed. I fought…to no avail.
Bittersweet.

Dots on the timeline of life.
Some dots difficult. Some dots dreamy.
And I am thankful for those dots.
But I am reminded of the line they melt together to form.
Such is life. Such is eternity.
There is the balance between cherishing the dots,
And recognizing the timeline.

I think back even farther:
Mary, the mother of Jesus.
She must have nestled her face into his hair.
She must have breathed in the fragrance
Of the sweet smelling hay on which he lay, perhaps,
And of the sweet fragrance of knowing…*HE* was *HIM*.
When she rested her hand on his back,
She must have felt the subtle rise and fall as He breathed.
Did she wonder how different this earthly air was...
Different from the heavenly air He had breathed?
As she listened to his quiet breathing…baby breaths…
Was she still for a moment?
Did Psalm 46:10 come to mind?
"Be still, and know that I AM GOD..." (KJV)
What comfort and awe that verse must have brought to her.
She was cradling the very *Son of GOD*…
GOD in the flesh.
Did she try to hold onto the moments?
Hold on…while knowing she would have to let go.
As her face brushed against His soft petal skin,
Was she reminded that *HE* Himself created the petals, the flowers, the *ALL*?
He breathed the earth into existence.
And now…the Word was made flesh,
And dwelt among us.

As she looked into His gentle face…did she immediately see something deeper?
Did she see the face of her gentle Shepherd?
Did she see the face of her Savior?
I wonder…as she listened to Him breathe.
I wonder…did the sound take *HER* breath away?
I wonder if…in that moment…
She sensed that eternity was encircled in her embrace?

The line.
Eternity…the line that had no beginning.
The line that will have no end.
We value the dots.
But we know that with God, the dots and the line merge.
With Him, time is insignificant.
And, we lose sight of what is truly valuable if we forget.
We cannot forget.

I wanted to hold onto childhood…
I could not.
I let go.
And I found out that being a Mommy is better!
I wanted to hold onto the childhoods of my own children.
I could not.
I let go.
And I discovered the joy of grand parenting.

I want to hold on to a lot of things.
I cannot.
I must enjoy the dots…use the dots…cherish the dots.
All the time knowing that the never ending line is greater.
I must glance at the dots…but set my gaze on the eternal.

"But as for me,
I trust in You, O Lord.
I say, 'You are my God.'
My times are in Your hand…"
(Psalm 31:14, 15)

"What Was *THAT*??"

T-Ball Season!
Nathan is five years old!
He absolutely loves baseball!

I am so happy that I had my long zoom lens to photograph Nathan.
He was too far away!
From "behind the fence", I couldn't see the expressions on his face.
The shielding of his face by his baseball cap did not help!

As I looked through my photos later that evening,
I laughed and laughed.
The photos were better than the game!
After posting several on Facebook, I enjoyed the captions people added!

Nathan's team was in the outfield.
His hands and face express some of his thoughts.
"What was that? Are you kidding me? We should have had that!"
Thoughts I never would have known, if I had not zoomed in and focused on his expression,
With my "long lens".

God has a *"long lens"*.
His lens zooms into the very center of our beings!
1 Samuel 16:7 tells us:
"...Man looks at the outward appearance, but the Lord looks at the heart."
We can fool man, but we cannot fool God.
He never has to stand "behind the fence".
We cannot shield ourselves from Him!

He sees our very thoughts!

2 Chronicles 16:9 is an "eye opener" for us:
"For the eyes of the Lord move to and fro throughout the earth
That He may strongly support
Those whose heart is completely His."

God is looking for a heart that is completely His.
His focus is on the very core of my inner being.
His eyes zoom into my heart and see my thoughts and intentions.

We can deceive others with our words and actions.
Even those closest to us do not know our motives.
We can even deceive ourselves into thinking we are right when we are wrong.

BUT GOD!!!
HE cannot be deceived, for He knows the Truth.

Do we have loyal hearts that are looking to Him?
Do we have clean hearts that are committed to Him?
Do we have dedicated hearts that we have fully given to Him?
If we do, He will show Himself strong on our behalf!
Lord, let it be!!

"SAVORED"

"Grandma, can we come see the kittens?"
Ah...baby kittens...
One of the signs of spring...
A reminder of new life...
A recurring source of joy for grandchildren!!

Marshall is the oldest of the grandchildren who still has an interest in kittens.
His two older brothers are beyond that stage.
Teenagers have "more important" things to do.
But Marshall...he is still in that middle school age...
And so...watching him with baby kittens brings me a special kind of heart smile.

Sometimes, there is a joy that is bittersweet...
A joy that is present because of the value of "the present"...
A joy that we hold onto as long as we can...
A joy that we try to strrrrreeeeetttttttttch.
We know that a much loved season is passing...
And so we hang on to the threads of that time.

I hold onto autumn, my favorite time of year.
The wind may have turned cold,
The air more brisk that I even like it.
But if there is just a thread of autumn color...
I will be breathing in the beauty of it.
I will be savoring every last moment...
Drawing out every possible bit of beauty this season of autumn has for me.
Relishing the "joy" it brings to my heart.

I did the same with my children.
I find myself doing the same with my grandchildren...
As they are passing into the next season of their lives...
In my heart...I hold onto the "threads".
I "breathe in" the beauty of the present.
I savor every precious moment...
I draw out every bit of joy this season of their lives has for me.

God's Word brings me a special kind of joy.

But this joy is not seasonal.
"...THE WORD OF THE LORD ENDURES FOREVER." (1 Peter 1:25)

How can we find joy in God's Word?
Psalm 1, verses one and two, tell us:
"How blessed is the man who does not walk in the counsel of the wicked,
Nor stand in the path of sinners,
Nor sit in the seat of scoffers!
But his DELIGHT is in the law of the Lord,
And in His law He MEDITATES day and night."

Do you *delight* in God's Word?
Do you take counsel from it?
Do you meditate on it?

The word, "meditate", is a unique word.
It was also used as a cow "chewing her cud".
A cow swallows her food, then brings it back up to chew over and over.
Meditate is to ponder…to think about over and over.
In a sense, it is the reverse of worry.
When we worry, we think about something distressing over and over.
When we meditate, we think about something precious or true…over and over.
If you can worry…you can meditate!!

What do you do when your mind is racing and won't relax?
What do you do when worries saturate your thoughts?
What do you do when sleep evades you?
Psalm 63, verses six, seven, and eight advise us,
"When I remember You on my bed,
I meditate on You in the night watches,
For You have been my help,
And in the shadow of Your wings I sing for joy.
My soul clings to You;
Your right hand upholds me."

Find a verse that speaks to your concerns.
Think about *EACH* word of that verse.
Ponder the meaning.
Let its truth melt into your heart.
Let it permeate into the very depths of your being.
It will transform your mind.

God's Word, our bread of life, "tastes" best when it is savored!
Jeremiah, in chapter 15, verse 16, says,
"Your words were found, and I ATE them.
And your words became for me a joy and the delight of my heart."

Assimilate His words into your very soul!
"Hold onto" them!
Cherish them!
Savor them!
They are *precious*!

"WEAK TO STRONG"

Once upon a time,
There was a sweet and saucy little girl.
Sweet...because she could capture my heart with a smile.
Saucy...because she had a *VERY* strong will...
AND she always wanted *EVERYTHING* to be *FAIR*!!!!

Her parents…and her teachers…
Were often puzzled…and frazzled…
Trying to teach this little "angel"
That life was NOT fair!
And she could not expect it to be.

——BUT GOD—-

One summer...
God captured this darling's heart...
And she started listening to *HIM*.

Gradually, *HE* taught her about fairness.
Life would never be fair, she learned.
But what did *HE* want her to do about that?
She started taking the focus off herself,
And placing it on others.
She immersed herself in God's Word...
His thoughts...His heart.

Counseling teens became her love.
She pursued social work in college.
Her internship?
Teaching young people...
How to live...when life is...
UNFAIR.

Bethany received her bachelor's degree… in social work.
We are excited to see where God will lead her.
We are confident that she will follow.
For...she has given her weaknesses to Him.
HER need for justice for herself
Has been replaced with Christ's strength
To minister to others when life is "unfair".

God has taught her...
"'...My grace is sufficient for you,
For power is perfected in weakness.'
Most gladly, therefore,
I will rather boast about my weaknesses,
So that the power of Christ may dwell in me.
Therefore, I am well content with weaknesses,
With insults, with distresses,
With persecutions, with difficulties,
For Christ's sake;
For when I am weak, then I am strong."
(2 Cor. 12: 9, 10)

Do you have a weakness?
Give it to God.
His grace is sufficient.
When you are weak…
HE is strong.

"LOOK-ALIKES"

Who do you "look like"?
When my grandson, Spencer, was four years old,
He and his Mom entered a "look alike" contest.
They won fourth place!
He still looks a lot like his Mom.
And he has a lot of his Mom's qualities...
They both are kind and caring and respectful.
They both have a way of making others smile and laugh.
They love the Lord and serve others.
Both volunteer in their community and help people in need.
Spencer is handsome...His Mom is beautiful!

Children often resemble their parents.
They are born with similar physical characteristics.
Over the years of training by a loving parent,
They often exhibit similar inner qualities.

God made man "in His image".
But sin took its toll.
By God's grace, His Son took the penalty for our sin.
A person who places his trust in Christ as Savior is "born again".
He gets to "start over" as a "new creation":
"Therefore if anyone is in Christ, he is a new creature;
The old things passed away; behold, new things have come."
-2 Corinthians 5:17-

Then, a wonderful process begins.
God works in His children to "grow them up".
Romans 8:29 tells us:
"For those whom He foreknew,
He also predestined to become conformed to the image of His Son..."

God, the Father, wants us to take on the characteristics of Christ.
Jesus came as "God in the flesh".

He said..."*I and the Father are one.*" *(John 10:30)*
He showed us God..."God with skin on".

I want to be like Him.
I want to see through His eyes....
Not seeing just surface issues, but real needs.
I want to hear through His ears...
Not just hearing words, but hearing the hurt behind the words.

My prayer?
"Lord, give me *Your* heart.
Conform me to *Your* image.
May I take on *Your* characteristics,
May I look like *You*. "

"STANDING TOGETHER"

Autumn has been beautiful this year.
The colors have been brilliant.
The weather has been sunny and cool.
The leaves are "hanging on" even in late October.
But, the day is drawing near...
Cold rain and wind will tear at the trees.
Leaves will fight to stay in place.
Most will fall!

I took a stroll through a nearby cemetery recently.
I was thankful to see the beauty, for the season is passing.
The trees surrounding the acreage were bright with color.
BUT...there was one…
One in the midst of the cemetery...
Whose leaves were nearly non-existent…
They had fallen to the ground.

I contemplated...why??
It was one of the larger and more stalwart trees.
The answer?

No trees stood near to hug against it.
No branches from another intertwined with its branches.
It was more susceptible to wind and rain.
As magnificent as it was, it stood alone.

Hebrews was written to believers who were facing adversity.
Persecution was at the door.
Many were tempted to "give up".
In the midst of instructions on "holding fast"...
Hebrews 10:25 says,
"Not forsaking our own assembling together,

As is the habit of some,
But encouraging one another;
And all the more as you see the day drawing near."

WE NEED EACH OTHER.
God's plan is that we encourage other believers.
HE ordained the church. It was *HIS* idea!
We *MUST* not think that we can stand alone.
Even the "strong" need support.

Find a church where Jesus Christ is preached.
Make fellowship with other believers a priority.
Christ died and rose again, providing salvation from our sins.
Faith in Him is the only way to Heaven.
The world is rejecting His message.

More and more believers are being persecuted for their faith.
The cold rain and wind tear and howl against us.
We feel threatened.

We must support and encourage each other.
We must not *give up*.
We must not fall.
We must build up each other in our faith.

HOLD FAST.
Be an encourager.
Attend church faithfully.
Support other believers.
To stand strong, we must stand together.

"THE TODDLER TWIST"

Caroline is two years old.
She has a special way of making the ordinary extraordinary.
A walk becomes a dance.
Washing hands evolves into a game of "slippery soap".
Taking a picture gives an opportunity to lovingly hug a tree!
I call this ability the "toddler twist".

Caroline's twist on life is especially apparent in her words!
When she first started talking, she called me "Gobba".
Gobba Juice was orange juice in a special sippy cup.
A cup found only at Gobba's house!
"Gobba" progressed into "Gomma",
Which became "Gamma", and then, "Gramma".
She still asks for "Gobba Juice", though!

One night, we were sitting around a campfire.
Caroline's Mommy was teaching her about "names".
After hearing our names only once…
She pointed at me and said, "Gramma's name…Joyce."
Then, she pointed at my husband, and said, "Grampa's name…Al."

Now, to be honest, I have never really liked my name,
Or my husband's name.
But…just add the "toddler twist".
Caroline's way of saying, "Aaal" is too cute!
And her twist on "Joyce" makes my name unique and special.

God has a special name, too!
Christendom calls Him, "Father".

After all, He is our Creator!
"For in Him we live and move and exist." (Acts 17:28)

Did you know that Jesus had another name for His Father?
In the Garden of Gethsemane, He called Him, *"Abba, Father"*.
"Abba" was a common way that young Jewish children addressed their fathers.
It conveyed that special family intimacy…that closeness,
Perhaps similar to "Daddy" or "Papa".
Did you also know that, as believers, we can address God as *"Abba, Father"*?
Why would our Creator desire such intimacy?
Because…we are His dearly loved children!

John 1 tells of God's coming to earth through His Son, Jesus.
It speaks of those who rejected Him…as God and as Savior.
But, the good news is given in verse twelve.
*"But as many as received Him, to them He gave the right to become
Children of God, even to those who believe in His name."*

Reject or receive? That is the question.
It is as though Jesus stands at the door of our hearts, knocking.
To ignore Him is to reject Him.
To say in our hearts,
"Come in, Jesus…thank you for dying for my sin…
Come and be my Savior and stay with me forever."
The moments our hearts believe in such a manner, we are born again.
We become a child of God.

I remember when I first received Jesus as my Savior.
I knew I had a new relationship with Him.
When I prayed, for the very first time in my life,
I knew I was praying to a loving, caring Father.
I did not understand, at the time, about all that had happened at that moment,
Galatians 4:6 says, *"Because you are sons,
God has sent forth the Spirit of His Son into our hearts, crying,
'Abba! Father!'"*
Romans 8:15 exclaims, *"…but you have received a spirit of adoption as sons
By which we cry out, 'Abba, Father!'"*

I was as a newborn babe.
And, in a kind of "toddler twist",
The language of my heart had changed.
I could now address God with that sense of family intimacy and closeness.
He was my Father. He was my Daddy.
I would forever be His child.

Are you His forever child?
Is He your, *"Abba, Father"*?
Welcome Him into your heart today.
Receive Him as Your Savior.
He will receive you as His child.

*CONTENTMENT
TO MELT THE
DISSATISFIED HEART*

"HELD"

A few weeks ago, my husband and I had a wonderful privilege!
We had the joy of watching our youngest grandson, "CJ"!
CJ and his big sister, Caroline, had a grand time!
Well...for the first hour anyway!
Something went wrong...we have yet to figure out what!

C J started crying!
Grandma and Grandpa tried everything to console him...
To no avail.
Finally, I just held him, and walked him back and forth...
Back and forth across the room...
Singing to him, "Jesus Loves Me"...over and over!

Finally...shortly before Mommy and Daddy walked in...
CJ calmed down and stopped crying.
Mommy's return was welcomed by all...especially her son.
She took him in her arms and spoke gently to him.
She sat down and just held him close.
She hugged him, and he melted in her embrace.
He was now content.

Ah...the satisfaction and security that comes from "Mommy".
A child who is loved senses that compassionate heart.
He thrives under the care of the "Mommy heart".

It has been said that the love of a mother
Is second only to the love of God.
In Isaiah 49: 15, 16, God speaks to His chosen people:

*"Can a woman forget her nursing child
And have no compassion on the son of her womb?
Even these may forget,
But I will not forget you.
Behold, I have inscribed you on the palms of My hands..."*

Sometimes, when we are hurting...
When the tears are flowing freely...
When it seems like God has forgotten us...
We need to remember the strength of God's love and compassion.
He does not forget!

James 4:8 says, *"Draw near to God and He will draw near to you."*
Go to Him!
Climb into His lap.
Pour out your heart.
He will listen to you.
He will dry your tears.
He will speak gently to you.
He will hold you close.
Rest…content…in His embrace.

*"Do not fear, for I am with you;
Do not anxiously look about you, for I am your God.
I will strengthen you,
Surely I will help you,
Surely I will uphold you with my righteous right hand."* -Isaiah 41:10-

"~~~STATIC HAIR~~~"

Static electricity is a strange phenomenon.
It is especially manifested during the dry, cold months of winter.
Dry hair tends to have positive electrical charges.
Therefore, strands of hair repel each other.
The hair strands stand up and try to push away from each other.

On this particular cold, wintry day, Caroline was visiting.
Going to Grandma and Grandpa's house became a "shocking" experience.
When she touched something, she was apt to get a shock, or "sharp" in Caroline language.
As she ran back and forth across the rug, her fine hair became quite the "electric" sight.
We had a lot of fun laughing and taking pictures!

So....if you are in the middle of winter...
I thought I would share some of our laughter with you.
We can use a "comic break".
A break from the snow shoveling and snow plowing...
A warm moment during the below zero temperatures of recent days.

So......laugh!
I mean....all that blonde static hair does look pretty funny!
After all...Proverbs 17:22 says, *"A joyful heart is good medicine."*
We could all use some "medicine" for our souls on some of these frigid days.

Enjoy some winter moments.
My husband finds joy in feeding the birds during the winter months.
He places value on even the little sparrows.

Remember God's concern for sparrows?
Luke 12:6, 7 tell us:
"Are not five sparrows sold for two cents?
Yet not one of them is forgotten before God.
Indeed the very hairs of your head are all numbered.
Do not fear;
You are more valuable than many sparrows."

Use the picture of Caroline's "static joy"...
To remind you of the great value God places on you!!
After all.....look at that hair!
And remember..."*the very hairs of your head are all numbered*".
Only *GOD* could know how many hairs are on your head.....even static hair!

"HEY...WHEN IS MY PARTY?"

"Hi Everybody!!
My name is CJ...and I am extreeeeemely upset!
You see...today is MY birthday.
And I would like to know just one thing...
WHEN IS MY PARTY?
I am dressed and ready...
"Birthday Boy" shirt and all...
So...what is the big hold-up?
I heard Mom and Dad talking about it...
So I know it is happening...
BUT...it is getting late, and guess what?
NO PARTY!!!!!
I AM VEEEERRRRY FRUSTRATED!!!!! "

Ha ha...did you ever wonder what your child was thinking?
It was CJ's birthday.
Mommy had taken him to the park...
He had swung in the baby swing...
He had played in the sand...
He should have been content...
But...observe the look on his face!
What is he thinking?

Mommy and Daddy had the party all planned.
CJ was going to have a great time outside...
With his family and friends...
Eating cake...
Getting presents...
Playing with his new toys...
Standing in the sprinkler...
Laughing and having a great time...
BUT...rain was on the way...

Party postponed for a week...
Patience required!!

When do we need patience?
Do we get upset and grouchy when we must wait?
Wait for something we want NOW?

Can we trust in God's timing?
Can we rest in His love and faithfulness?
Do *WE KNOW* that *HE KNOWS* all things?
HIS ways are higher than our ways...
HIS thoughts are higher than our thoughts?
Can we be *STILL* and *KNOW* that *HE IS GOD*?

Does frustration cause us to push OUR ways?
Do we press OUR timing,
And then complain when it "rains on our parade"?

Lack of patience is a symptom of lack of trust...
Whether it be a little thing...like a slooooow car ahead of me...
Or a lifetime thing...like a marriage partner...
Can we trust GOD?

How about eternal issues?
Jesus knew that we would be tempted to be troubled.
The night before He died to pay for our sins, He said,
"Do not let your heart be troubled;
Believe in God, believe also in Me.
In My Father's house are many dwelling places;
If it were not so, I would have told you;
For I go to prepare a place for you.
If I go and prepare a place for you,
I will come again and receive you to Myself,
That where I am, there you may be also."
(John 14:1-3)

Jesus made a promise to return!
Years later, in 2 Peter 3, these words are recorded:
"...*In the last days, mockers will come...*
...*Saying, 'Where is the promise of His coming...?'* "

The Lord warned us that there would be scoffers...
Those who would use the "delay" to make fun of us...
But God has the answer...
"Do not let this one fact escape your notice, beloved,
THAT WITH THE LORD
ONE DAY IS LIKE A THOUSAND YEARS,
AND A THOUSAND YEARS LIKE ONE DAY.
The Lord is not slow about His promise, as some count slowness,

*But is patient toward you,
Not wishing for any to perish but for all to come to repentance."*

As believers in Christ,
We must look at things from His eternal perspective.
The book of Hebrews was written to persecuted believers...
Followers of Christ who were under pressure to "give up"...
The author, in chapter 10, encouraged them, saying,
*"...Do not throw away your confidence, which has a great reward,
For you have need of ENDURANCE,
So that when you have done the will of God,
You may receive what was promised.
FOR YET, IN A VERY LITTLE WHILE,
HE WHO IS COMING WILL COME,
AND WILL NOT DELAY."*

How, then, do we live?
God tells us, in the next verse...
"BUT MY RIGHTEOUS ONE SHALL LIVE BY FAITH."
FAITH...KNOWING that what God says is true...
God's Word has always been true...is true...will always be true!!
We can count on it!!
HE KEEPS HIS PROMISES!!

Christ could return at any moment...
When? I do not know....He did not tell us.
But...this I do know...
*HE WILL RETURN!
AND ...IT WILL BE WORTH THE WAIT!*

Meditation Moments To Melt The Heart

"I am so happy! It's time for my party!!!"

"Ahhhhh…worth the wait!"

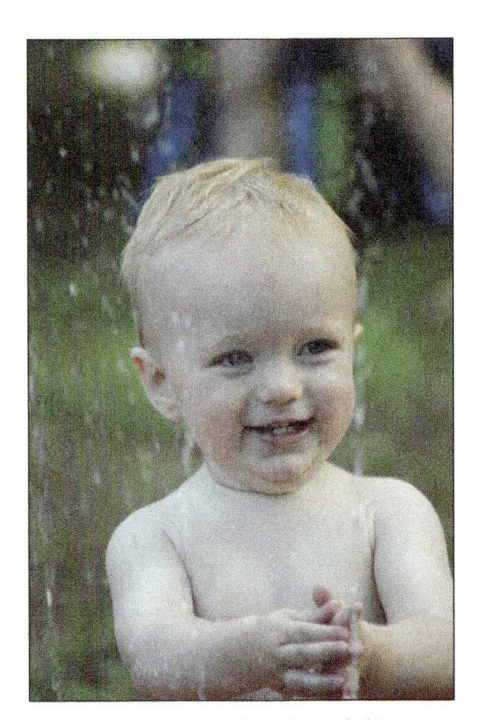

"Yep…I do prefer this sprinkler over rain!"

"DEFINITELY WORTH THE WAIT!!!"

"WHAT HAPPENED?"

My Mom had reams of jewelry.
Much of it, she crafted!
My granddaughters love to play with her costume jewelry.

A few weeks ago, Caroline discovered the necklaces.
One by one, she picked up each treasure.
One by one, she oohed and aahed over the colors.
One by one, she placed each one around her neck.
Soon, she looked like the queen of the necklace!
She played and admired all her magnificence...UNTIL...

It was time to remove each necklace.
They had become entangled.
Caroline was no longer happy.
The jewelry she had admired became a burden to her.
She wanted them OFF!!

Grandma to the rescue!
We removed the tangled mess!
Caroline was free...and content to be "necklace-free"!

Hebrews 12:1 and 2 remind us not to become "entangled"!
"...Let us also lay aside every encumbrance
And the sin which so easily entangles us,
And let us run with endurance the race that is set before us,
Fixing our eyes on Jesus, the author and perfecter of faith..."

The deception of Satan and of sin surround us.
Satan disguises himself as an "angel of light".
He makes the detrimental look delicious.
And so, we are enticed!

"Just this once I will_____."
"I will try just one_____."
"Surely, one _____ won't hurt me."
You fill in the blanks.
Soon, we discover that all the oohs and aahs of each "one"...
Have served to entangle us in a "mess"!
We want out!!!

I will never forget a message given by Harry Bollback,
Co-founder of *Word of Life Fellowship*.
That particular message, applying Heb. 12:1 and 2,
Has influenced many of my decisions for forty five years!

Mr. Bollback, during a typical northern snowstorm,
Had traveled to a meeting via snowmobile.
As he entered the building, he was asked to play the organ.
An accomplished musician, Mr. Bollback quickly agreed.
As the strains of organ music began to fill the room,
He became aware of a problem!
He was still wearing his snow mobile boots!
Such an encumbrance prevented him from using the pedals!!
What did he do???
He removed the snow mobile boots!!!!!

What are *YOUR* "snow mobile boots"?
What "weight" is keeping you from "running the race"?
A "weight" or "encumbrance" may not be a sin.
A successful runner does *MORE* than just "keep the rules".
He/she removes any unnecessary weights!

Each of us is tempted in different ways!
Shopping can be enjoyable.
However, a preoccupation with accumulating material goods,
Causes us to lose focus on what is important!
TV can be good...but too much...or the wrong programs??
Video games and apps are fun! But too many waste time…
Time God wants us to use wisely!
And the list goes on........

Whether it be a deliberate sin... lying, cheating, stealing...
Or something "innocent" that is holding us back from God's will...
We can become entangled.
We find ourselves focused on the tangled mess,
Instead of keeping our eyes on the goal!!

How do we run this race??
Lay aside the weights!
Lay aside the sin!
Fix your eyes on Jesus!
Christ is able to remove the tangled mess!
HE will set you free!

"CONTENT?"

Grandma had just given CJ a toddler cup...
A cup full of tasty, cold, nutritious milk.
CJ usually loves his milk…
But not today!

My adorable, sweet, seventeen month old grandson had a better idea.
He turned the cup upside down,
And proceeded to shake its contents out of the spout...
All over himself and his surroundings!
What a mess Grandma had to clean up!

Shortly after this scenario, CJ noticed something.
Grandma had set her coffee mug on the coffee table.
He gingerly walked over to the mug and just stared at it.
Periodically, he looked up…
Then, he toddled closer.
He bent over and gazed into the mug.
He looked up.
Then...he placed his head as close as he could to that mug…
His face was almost touching the rim.
He just peered into the mug for the longest time.
It appeared that he was longing for the contents of that cup...
Wanting what Grandma had...
Desiring something perhaps...in his thoughts...better than milk...
Not understanding that coffee was not healthy for him.
It was also not at a "toddler temperature".
Although he may like the appearance ...he would not like the taste.
And the mug was much too large...and heavy...for him!
He would have to wait until he was older...and taller...and ready for coffee!

This past Thanksgiving...most of us expressed our thanks.
We thanked God for family...and friends...and possessions.
Our hearts were blessed and we wanted to bless God.
I wonder if we can keep that thankful heart all year.

How long will it take us to start complaining?
How many days can we go without whining?
How long before we feel the need to "keep up with the Joneses"?

Do we sit outside the Jones' home and stare?
Do we look up to God and expect what "the Joneses" have?
Do we walk up the sidewalk and gaze upon the beauty of it all...
And look up and wish it was all ours?
Do we put our faces against their windows and peer through the glass?
Do we long for the possessions we see and want what they have?

Desiring the possessions of another is not uncommon...
It may be a house or a car...
Or it may be...
"I wish my family was like the McDougal family"...
Or, "I wish my husband was like Matilda's husband"...
Or, "I wish my kids were like Maria's kids"...
All thoughts of discontent and coveting.
Remember these words from the Tenth Commandment, recorded in Exodus 20:17:
"You shall not covet your neighbor's house;
You shall not covet your neighbor's wife...
Or anything that belongs to your neighbor."

Contentment often begins where coveting ends...
When we trust that every gift is from our *All* Knowing Father...
Designed for us alone...no one else,
By His loving and gracious hand.

CJ did not understand that the coffee he wanted was not right for him.
It was not better than the milk that was designed for his needs.
Perhaps, coffee will never be "right" for him...
Perhaps, it will.
But...at this time in his life...it is not!
If he was given coffee...he would very soon discover this truth.
Although it looks good...
Although it smells good...
Although it appears to be what he wants...
If he actually ingests it...
He will quickly realize that the taste and the temperature are not to his liking.
He will find out that the mug is too heavy...
He may even drop it on his toes and get hurt.
At the very least, he will hand it back to me.
The disgusted look on his face will say...
"Please...take it away...I don't like it after all... Give me milk!"

The sad thing is...
Once we have turned upside down the blessings God has given us...
Once we have shaken them up and thrown them away...
Once we have soaked ourselves and those around us with our selfishness...
It may be too late to gather up those blessings and put them back.

Thankfully...God is full of forgiveness and grace.
He can take our brokenness and remold us.
He will bless us again.
But the path we have left behind us...
Strewn with blessings we have tossed aside...
May take many years to reclaim.

The apostle Paul, in Philippians 4:11-13, tells us...
"...I have learned to be content in whatever circumstances I am.
I know how to get along with humble means,
And I also know how to live in prosperity...
I can do all things through Him who strengthens me."

Contentment knows God has and will supply exactly what is best for me.
So...be content.
A content heart is not always groping for something better.
It is resting in the God who provides all I need.

"LOVED AND SECURE"

I loved being a "Mommy" of little ones.
The joy I experienced then...is rivaled by the joy I experience now.
I watch...as my adult "little ones"...
Now mother their own little ones.
My heart sings as I observe the deep love they share.

One of a Mom's goals is to bring security to her child.
Warm hugs are spontaneous and frequent.
I love the picture above:
Mommy is lifting Nate and holding him close.
And Ella, craving the same attention…
Is snuggled up to Mom and clinging to her...
Smiling in her shadow.

Our Heavenly Father is the Ultimate Parent.
He wants us to be secure in His love.
He lifts us up and holds us.
We can cling to Him.
We can sing in His shadow!

"For You have been my help, And in the shadow of Your wings I sing for joy.
My soul clings to You; Your right hand upholds me."
-Psalm 63: 7, 8-

As God's child...You are loved.
You are secure. You are *HIS!*

"FORGOTTEN?"

"Grandma...do you know what I want for my birthday?
I want a big, soft, cuddly stuffed dog!"
I didn't know such an animal would be so difficult to find.
I had to tell Ella I was sorry, but I had been unable to find one.
She had been so sweet, reassuring me that it was ok.
That was March 2013.

December 2013...Christmas time...
Again, I was hoping to find that soft cuddly creature.
To no avail.

February 2014...
I was walking through a grocery store.
There on the shelf, to my excited surprise, was the dog...
The exact dog I knew Ella would love.
It was big and soft and cuddly...and even had pink trimmings,
Which made it ideal for Princess Ella.
I took it home and hid it in my closet!

March 2014...
Ella's birthday party.
The dog was wrapped in a big box.
It had been so long that Ella didn't even suspect...
Until it popped out of the box at her.
She giggled and smiled and hugged the dog...and me!
What a great surprise, made even more special because of the long wait.
Grandma had not forgotten!
She had just been delayed.

How do we react when our prayers seem unanswered?
We all know that God *WILL* answer...

Yes or No or Wait.
We continue to pray and wonder and ask and wait.
There are times when we just place our request at the feet of Jesus...
And we leave it there,
Trusting Him!

But God is *ALWAYS* at work!
He never forgets our prayers and our needs.
We can depend on Him.

In Daniel 10, Daniel had an amazing experience.
All had appeared like God was not answering a request he had made.
But, in this chapter, we catch a glimpse of God's "behind the scenes" activity.
Daniel had prayed and fasted for three weeks.
God seemed to be silent.
Then, an angel appeared.

The angel assured Daniel that, from the first day, his words had been heard.
God had not ignored him.
The angel said,
"Do not be afraid, Daniel,
For from the first day that you set your heart on understanding this
And on humbling yourself before your God,
Your words were heard,
And I have come in response to your words." (Daniel 10:12)

What took Him so long?
Verse 13 gives the answer.
"But the prince of the kingdom of Persia was withstanding me for twenty one days..."
Apparently, a satanic adversary had fought with him,
And kept him from delivering the answer for twenty one days.

God had not forgotten.
The answer had been "on its way" all along.
God was at work.
Daniel received his answer.

In Matthew 7:7, 8, Jesus tells his disciples,
"Ask, and it will be given to you;
Seek, and you will find;
Knock, and it will be opened to you.
For everyone who asks receives;
And he who seeks finds;
And to him who knocks it will be opened."

The Greek language in which these verses were written, actually implies:
Ask...and keep on asking.
Seek...and keep on seeking.
Knock...and keep on knocking.

Never give up!
God hears your prayers...always.
He answers your prayers...always.
He does not forget.
Perhaps, the answer will come today!
Or, perhaps, someday in the future, you will open a gift He has given,
And, in your spirit, it will seem like God is saying,
"Surprise!"
And you will know that, because you waited...because you trusted...
He has given you more than you could ask or imagine!
God remembered!
And the answer was worth your wait!

"Now to him who is able to do
FAR MORE ABUNDANTLY BEYOND
All that we ask or think,
According to the power that works within us,
To him be the glory in the church
And in Christ Jesus
To all generations
Forever and ever.
Amen."
(Ephesians 3: 20 and 21)

"THE VALUE OF THE ONE"

Unique!!
Special!!
Set apart from all the rest!!

It always amazed me...
The vast differences between our children.
And now?
The vast differences between our grandchildren!

Mary is our animal lover!
She is drawn to them...and they to her.
She has no aspirations to become a lion trainer.
She doesn't want to lead a safari.
But give her one frightened kitten and she will console it.
Wake her up in the morning,
And you will see one little dachshund peek out from under her blanket.
Both of them look at me with that...
"Not yet...we're cuddling" stare!

I wonder why, as we get older, we lose that easy "satisfaction".
We start aspiring to be the best,
The highest at the chain of command,
The one with the biggest house,
Or the shiniest car.
And, as we do, we become dissatisfied with life.
After all, there is always someone with more money,
More possessions, more power, more prestige.

Sadly, such complications spill over into our spiritual lives.
We want to be the one "in charge".

We want to attend the biggest church.
We want to have the most followers.
Instead of wisely using the gifts and talents God has given to us,
And encouraging others to become all God created *THEM* to be,
We try to "do it all".
Spiritual pride sets in.
Our lives become busy, but lose deep significance.

God has been reminding me of the value of simplicity.
Simply being who He made me to be...
Simply walking with Him...
Wherever that walk may lead me....or not lead me.
For *HE* values what, to us, sometimes may seem insignificant.
He values the "One"!

In Luke 15, Jesus gives examples of the value of one.
"What man among you, if he has a hundred sheep and has lost ONE of them,
Does not leave the ninety-nine in the open pasture
And go after the one which is lost until he finds it?" (v. 4)
"Or what woman, if she has ten silver coins and loses ONE coin,
Does not light a lamp and sweep the house
And search carefully until she finds it?" (v. 8)
"In the same way, I tell you,
There is joy in the presence of the angels of God
Over ONE sinner who repents." (v. 10)

Perhaps today, God wants me to focus on ONE.
Perhaps He wants me to do a seemingly "insignificant" task.
Perhaps He wants me to offer one word of encouragement.
I must simply trust Him and follow His path…
One *valuable* step at a time.

CLARITY

TO MELT THE

DOUBTING HEART

"WALK IN LOVE"

There is something special about the bond between siblings.
They may annoy each other...on purpose.
They may bicker and be "bossy".
They may take different paths as they grow older.
But...deep in their hearts...
There is a connection...
A bond formed through the "glue" of family.
An understanding that comes from being raised in the same household…
Loved...or not loved...by the same parents.

Our second daughter is Mommy to three beautiful children.
I am thankful that I am able to spend time with them weekly.
They are typical siblings.
They do not always get along...
But they always watch out for each other.

I love the above image...
Not only because it as a sweet picture of my grandchildren.
I love it because it is a picture of sibling love and caring.
Mary, the oldest, could have run ahead of her brother and sister.
But, she didn't!
She reached out, grabbed their hands,
And walked with them down the path.

The photo also reminds me of the bond between *God's* children.
Those who have trusted God's Son as Savior...
Have been born into God's family.
We have the same loving Heavenly Father.

Romans 5:5 tells us, *"...the love of God has been poured out within our hearts*
Through the Holy Spirit who was given to us."
We have been given the Spirit of God to dwell within us.

We have a connection that cannot be broken.
We have a bond!

Colossians 3:14 says,
"Beyond all these things put on love, which is the perfect bond of unity."
The "glue" that holds us together is the love of family.
God is our Father...and HE IS LOVE!
We are His children.

Over 2000 years ago, God "reached out His hands to us".
Jesus Christ left the glories of Heaven and walked on this earth.
Instead of receiving Him,
We nailed those holy hands to a cross.
And now, those nail scarred hands continue to reach out to us.
Those scars show the evidence of His love...
He paid for our sin.
When we place our sin-scarred hands into His nail-scarred hands...
When we place our trust in HIM...
He forgives our sins and declares us to be His children.

Ephesians 5:1, 2 tell us...
Therefore be imitators of God, as beloved CHILDREN;
And WALK IN LOVE,
Just as Christ also has loved you
And gave Himself up for us..."

Jesus Christ is to be imitated.
We now, as His children, are asked to walk in love.
We are asked to reach out our hands to others...
To love and forgive...
To give of ourselves...
To encourage...
To walk through this life together.

Christian brothers and sisters may not always see "eye to eye"...
But they should always see "heart to heart".
For...within their hearts...dwells the same Jesus.

Christian "siblings" may take different paths in this life...
But they are always on the same narrow road...
They walk beside each other on the road to everlasting life in Jesus.

I reiterate the truth of my opening paragraph...
But, this time, I ask you to consider the family of God...
There is something special about the bond between siblings.
They may disagree from time to time.
They may take different paths in life.
But...deep in their hearts…
There is a connection...

A bond formed through the "glue" of family...
An understanding that comes from being in the same "household"...
Loved by the same Heavenly Father.

We were not created to "stand alone" in this life.
Christ is always with us.
He has given us "brothers and sisters".
Together...we walk.
Together...we work.
Together...we live out the love of our Lord.

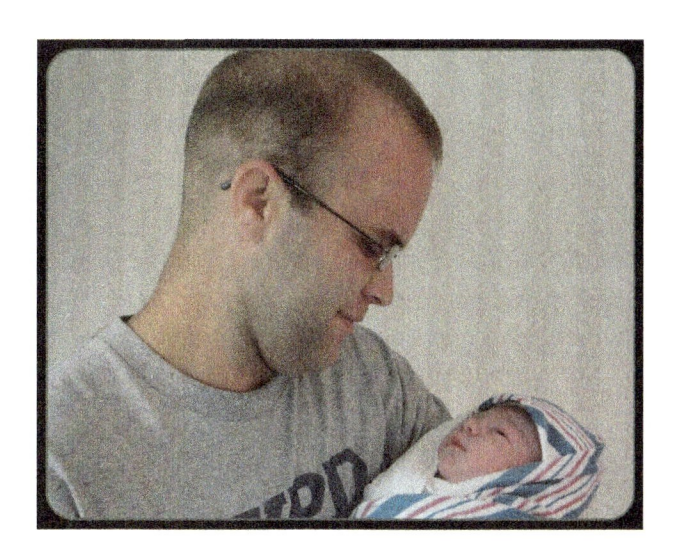

"FIRST LOOKS"

Watching...weighing...waiting...wrapping!
Nurses work...Daddy waits…
Waits to hold his newborn son!
Finally he reaches out and embraces this brand new life.
Daddy gazes at this newest gift from his God.

CJ opens his eyes!
He looks at the light ...a new, fresh look.
His Daddy is just beyond this new light.
Of course, he does not yet recognize him.
The baby is just beginning the process of learning to focus.
Someday...soon...he will recognize Daddy.
Opening his eyes to the light is the first step.

I wonder if there is a sense in which our "Heavenly Daddy" stands just beyond the light...
Waiting for someone to open his/her eyes.
Jesus said, *"I am the Light of the world." (John 8:12)*
He also said, *"No one comes to the Father but through Me." (John 14:6)*
If we want to see the Father, we must come through the Son.

In Luke 24:13ff, we read about two travelers.
They were journeying to Emmaus and discussing recent events in Jerusalem.
The crucifixion of Jesus.
The dashed hopes.
The claims that He was alive again.

*"While they were talking and discussing,
Jesus Himself approached and began traveling with them.
But their eyes were prevented from recognizing Him."*

He asked them about their conversation.
He saw their sadness.

They told him how the One they hoped would redeem Israel had been sentenced to death.
He saw their questioning spirits.
They told Him about those who had gone to the empty tomb.
He saw their doubts.

"And He said to them,
'O foolish men and slow of heart to believe in all that the prophets have spoken!
Was it not necessary for the Christ to suffer these things and to enter into His glory?' "
"Then beginning with Moses and with all the prophets, He explained to them
The things concerning Himself in all the Scriptures."

They still had not recognized Who He was.
They asked him to stay with them, for it was getting late.
When it was time to eat, *"He took the bread and blessed it,*
And breaking it, He began giving it to them."
"THEN THEIR EYES WERE OPENED AND THEY RECOGNIZED HIM"
They saw the Truth.
They believed!

Have your eyes been opened to recognize Him?
Have you seen the One who died for your sins?
He is alive!
The Heavenly Father waits for you to open your eyes to the Light!

Jesus said, *"And this is the will of Him who sent Me,*
That everyone who sees the Son and believes in Him
May have everlasting life;
And I will raise him up at the last day." (John 6:40, NKJV)

Have you seen the Son of God?
Open your eyes.
Take that first look!
Look to Him for your salvation!
Place your trust in Him.
Believe!!!

"GOODNIGHT MOON"

So bright! So beautiful! Almost magical!

I walked out of the hospital 3:30 A.M., Saturday morning. It was the middle of the night. My heart was filled with thanksgiving. I had just witnessed the birth of a beautiful baby boy...my sixth grandson. God is so good. Psalm 136:1 says, *"Give thanks to the Lord, for He is good, For His lovingkindness is everlasting."* Thank you, Lord, for my newest grandson! You are so good to us.

As I looked up at the sky ahead of me, I was amazed at the beauty of the full "blazing" moon! I have seldom seen the moon appear any more awe-inspiring. This piece of creation has become the subject of or symbol in much art, music, and literature. Even children's literature speaks of "the cow jumping over the moon", or "the man in the moon", or "Goodnight Moon".

Psalm 136 expresses a wonderful truth about the moon. The moon is given as one of the examples of God's mercy for which we should express thanks to our God. According to verse 9, He made, *"The moon and stars to rule by night, For His lovingkindness is everlasting."*

The word, "lovingkindness", in this verse, can also be translated, "loyal love" or "mercy". Isn't it great that we can always depend on the "loyal love" of our Lord? His mercy and love are everlasting. His love will never fail. He will always be there for me. He will always be there for my children. He will always be there for my grandchildren!

To a child, love is often spelled T-I-M-E. God is never too busy for us. Sadly, we are often "too busy" for those we love the most. I am so thankful that my new grandson has a Daddy who spends much time with his children. He is a busy man. He works fulltime, is enrolled in college classes, and gives of his time serving others. His children, however, take priority over all that busyness.

In 1974, Harry and Sandy Chapin published a song entitled, "Cat's in the Cradle". Its lyrics express the passage of time and the necessity of spending time with our children. He sings:

"My child arrived just the other day,
He came to the world in the usual way.
But there were planes to catch, and bills to pay.
He learned to walk while I was away.

And he was talking 'fore I knew it, and as he grew,
He'd say, 'I'm gonna be like you, dad.
You know I'm gonna be like you.'

And the cat's in the cradle and the silver spoon,
Little boy blue and the man in the moon,
'When you coming home, dad?'
'I don't know when,
But we'll get together then.
You know we'll have a good time then.' "

The song goes on to express the different times the dad and son could have spent together, but didn't. The tearful ending shows how the son did, indeed, become just like his dad. The retired dad calls his busy son, asking to see him. His response is, *"I'd love to, dad, if I could find the time..."*

One of the bedtime books that my daughter and son-in-law read to my granddaughter is, "Goodnight Moon", written by Margaret Wise Brown, in 1947, before I was born. It has been a staple in many homes for three generations. It is a refreshingly simple children's story. Reading books is one of the many activities we can do to spend quality time with our children.

Studies show that a child's concept of his/her Heavenly Father, is greatly affected by the influence of his/her earthly father. This understanding of the characteristics of God is often carried into adulthood. What are we teaching our children about the "loyal love" of our God?

So...parents and grandparents and aunts and uncles...next time you look at the moon, remember it is an example of the "loyal love" of God. And determine, in your heart, to take the time to show love to the children in your life. God always has "time" for us. He will not say, "Not now, I am busy." Granted, there are times we must use those words, but let those times be few. Time passes toooo quickly!

Well, back to 3:30 A.M., Saturday morning. I couldn't gaze at the moon for too long. I had to leave the hospital where my newest grandson had been born. I had to say, "Goodnight Moon"! I had to get some rest. For that same morning, at 10 A.M., my oldest grandson was graduating from high school. Time passes so quickly. The door to childhood is just opening for "CJ". It has already closed behind Ethan. We used to call him, "Ethie bear". We still do...sometimes. Is he really graduating from high school already? It wasn't that long ago that he was born. Was it???

"And the cat's in the cradle and the silver spoon,
Little boy blue and the man in the moon..."

"BLUEBERRY PICKIN'"

Ahhhhh....Blueberries!
The season has arrived.
Thankfully, my favorite berry is fun to harvest!

I have gone blueberry pickin' for a few years now.
My family laughs at me when I haul home gallons of berries to freeze!
But....I eat them nearly every day!!
I never get tired of them...
AND they are good for me!

The first few times I picked blueberries left me wondering...
Why didn't birds eat the berries before people could pick them?
As I wandered between the rows of bushes...
I could hear loud screeching and squawking!
Where were these squawkers?
Why didn't those hungry birds swoop down and have a feast?
Finally...I discovered the "secret"!

The local birds were actually afraid of approaching the blueberries!
Why???
The loud "screeching" that reverberated through the fields was deceptive!
It was loud! It was frightening!
BUT THE SQUAWKING WAS NOT REAL!!!
The recorded squawk of the hawk flowed through tiny boxes...
Boxes situated at appropriate intervals throughout the fields...
"Squawk Boxes" that terrorized the real birds!

I asked the Lord if there was a lesson He could teach me while pickin' berries.
And I wonder...
How many times have I been scared away from a blessing God had for me...
Frightened by my own perception of an event...
Terrified by the "squawking" of the Enemy...the "Deceiver"?
How often have I allowed fear to rob me?

Fear can penetrate so deeply into my soul that it smothers the truth.
The terror I feel overrides the ability to see what is real.
I do not realize that this "squawking" that is scaring me...
Is coming from empty boxes...

How sad that I am often the one who fills those boxes...
I fill them with a variety of deceptions...
False insecurities...
False accusations from others...
False emphasis on past failures...
False expectations...
False imaginations...
False intimidations...
False needs to please man over God...
And the list goes on...
All false...
All deceptions...
All producing squawkings that fill my heart with fear...
Fear that prevents me from pursuing what God has for me...
Fear that robs me of fruit...
Fear that robs me of blessing.

2 Timothy 1:7 *(NKJV)* is an encouraging verse:
"For God has not given us a spirit of fear,
But of power and of love and of a sound mind."

When I am afraid...I need to remember...
The spirit of fear is not from my Lord...
I need to use the sound mind He has given to me.
I need to listen to the Truth of God's Word.

It is through focusing on the Lord and His Word that I can overcome fear.
I can learn to recognize the lies.
I can fill my mind with what is true.

Through Christ, I can find the strength to stand on the Truth.
I can discover His will and pursue His plan.
I can "fill my bucket" with His blessings...
No matter how loud the "squawking" may be!!!

"KEEP YOUR EYE ON THE BALL"

CJ has a favorite toy.
Whenever he has the option, he will choose this one thing.
Can you guess what CJ's mind set is?
THE BALL!
He absolutely, irrevocably LOVES balls.
Little ones, large ones, old ones, new ones...always the ball.

"Keep your eye on the ball"... is CJ's motto.
One day, CJ carried a golf ball in his little hand ALL DAY.
He would not let it out of his sight.

When he comes to Gramma's house...he toddles to the toy box.
He proceeds to pull out ...you guessed it... the BALL.
He will willingly let go of the ball for one reason...
To play a game with the ball.

CJ's fascination with balls is fun to watch.
I never have to beg him to play with a ball.
I don't set up any rules demanding that he play with a ball.
He doesn't need to be cajoled...
He simply loves balls.
In his mind...they are wonderful!

So...what...or who...is wonderful in your mind?
What...or who...do *YOU* love?
If you have a choice, what...or who...comes first?
Where is *YOUR* mind set?

When I first understood how much Christ loved me...
So much that He died to pay for my sin and provide the way to Heaven...
I fell in love with Jesus...
1 John 4:19 *(NKJV)* exclaims:
"We love Him because He first loved us."
I placed my trust in Him and received Him into my heart.
I have never been the same.

You see...the Christian life is not about rules.
It is not a religion based on laws.
It is a relationship based on love.

When I became a Christian...God did not give me a list of rules to follow.
He gave me His Spirit to reside in me.
My heart...my mind...my life...all changed that day.
I HAVE HIM!

How, then, do I live?
I live...with *HIM* living in me.
Romans 8:6 tells us:
*"For the mind set on the flesh is death,
But the mind set on the Spirit is life and peace."*

The Christian life really is not as complicated as some think.
If I love the Lord Jesus...my mind will be set on Him.
I will be guided by Him.
He will live through me.
I will commune with Him.
I will experience real life.
I will have peace.

If I do not love Jesus...
My focus will be something else...something this world has to offer...
Something that I think will fill the void that only God's love can fill.
Something of the flesh...that will not last.
Something that will ultimately draw me away from the Lord who loves me...
Something that will bring separation from closeness with Him.
Something that will steal lasting peace...
Something that will make me a slave to sin...
Rather than a follower of my loving Lord.

So...the question is...
Do I love *HIM?*
Is He the first thing on my mind when I awaken?
Do I spend time with Him in His Word?
Is He my first choice?
Do I carry Him with me ...always aware of His presence?
Is He my all in all?

CJ's mind set is, "Keep your eye on the ball!"
Why? Because he absolutely, irrevocably loves balls.
He thinks they are wonderful!

What is my mind set?
May my motto ever be…
"Keep your mind on the Lord Jesus!"
Why? Because I absolutely, irrevocably love HIM!
He is my Wonderful Lord!

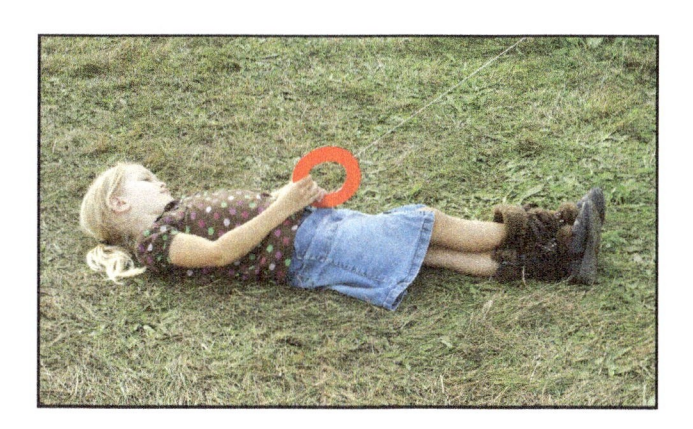

"AT REST"

Finally...the kite was flying high!
Mom and Grampa and Caroline had accomplished their goal!
Caroline was delighted!!

She stood for a few minutes, string in hand.
Then, she sat!
Then, she lay down!

People walked by and peered at her.
Cars slowly came and went via a nearby lane.
Daddy stood next to her.
I heard her quietly say, "Daddy, am I ok?"

"Yes, you're ok," he responded.
"I am watching out for you."

In all my years of watching kites fly...
I have never seen the person on the other end of the string so secure!
Secure enough to quietly rest!!
Caroline was confident that her kite would continue to soar...
And it did!

In chapter 30 of the book of Isaiah, the Heavenly Father exhorted His people.
Verse 15 *(KJV)* says,
"For thus saith the Lord God, the Holy One of Israel;
In returning and rest shall ye be saved;
In quietness and in confidence shall be your strength:
And ye would not."

We are not saved because of what we have done.
We are saved because the Lord Jesus has died to take away our sins.
He has sent the "wind" of the Holy Spirit to give us that salvation.
He has placed the "string" of faith in our hands.
Faith is the connection.
Faith can be understood as a rest, a "lying down on the inside".

Faith is a rest that is based on confidence in a Person.
It is not blind. It sees the Truth. It rests in the Truth.

Caroline could lie down and fly a kite.
She was secure in the power of the wind to keep up the kite.
She was secure in the presence of her Daddy to care for her.
She could rest...quietly and confidently.

And me? My soul?
Sometimes, I find "resting" difficult.
I struggle to be still.
I struggle to "lie down on the inside"...
Until I remember the power of God;
Until I rest in the presence of God.

I grasp on to the string of faith.
I trust in the Son of God who died for me.
I rely on His Holy Spirit and the truth of His Word.
I trust in the presence of my Heavenly Father.
And, periodically, I say, "Daddy, am I ok?"

His assurance comforts me.
"Yes, you're ok. I'm watching out for you."

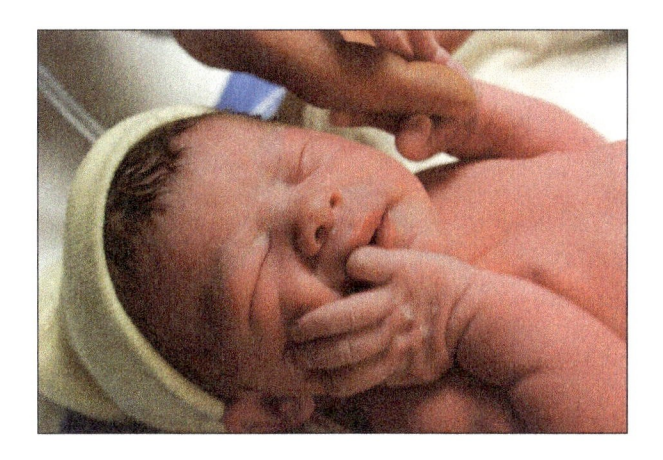

"MAY I INTRODUCE YOU..."

The long awaited call had come...
"We need to go to the hospital *NOW!*"
I quickly got ready and rushed to the car.
As I drove down the driveway,
My car's audio system clicked on.

The words I heard?
"May I Introduce You to this friend of mine..."
I smiled...inside and out!
I felt like I was hearing a comforting message.
God was going to introduce us to this baby. All was well.

Addison Grace was born a few hours later.
What a beautiful baby she is!
What a gift of grace from the Lord!

My Facebook status that evening read like this:
"Blessed....so blessed!
Amazingly blessed to be with Tabitha and Richard
As they welcomed Addison Grace into this world.
God is so faithful!
So many prayers were answered by our *LORD* who is full of Grace!
Tears and joy and so much *LOVE*!
Thank you, Lord!
YOU are faithful...throughout all generations.
What a special kind of joy to hear our beautiful and happy daughter
Hum the song, "Jesus Loves Me", to her new baby girl....
Flashback to when I sang the same song to her forty years ago!!
Oh my...God's love never changes!
I am in love....again!"

In Jeremiah 1:5, we read God's words to that prophet:
"Before I formed you in the womb I knew you,
And before you were born I consecrated you..."

God knew and set apart Jeremiah for a purpose...
Before he was even born.
The same is true of all His children.
The same is true of Addison Grace.

The words I heard that morning were...
"May I introduce you to this friend of mine..."
My prayer is that Addison will be God's friend.

In John 15: 14 and 15 *(NKJV)*, Jesus spoke to his disciples:
"You are my friends if you do whatever I command you.
No longer do I call you servants,
For a servant does not know what his master is doing;
But I have called you friends,
For all things that I heard from my Father
I have made known to you."

What is the difference between a servant and a friend?
A servant does what he is told.
A friend has a relationship...
A relationship based on love and trust and communication.

I know that Jesus *is MY* friend.
BUT...Am I *HIS* friend?
In the Bible, Abraham is named as a friend of God.
James 2:23 *(NKJV)* says,
"...'Abraham believed God, and it was accounted to him for righteousness,'
And he was called the friend of God."
Abraham believed God's promises and trusted *HIM* totally...
His steadfast *OBEDIENCE* was forged from an unfaltering *FAITH*!

What a wonderful privilege...
To be called a friend of God!
But only those who enter into deep fellowship with God have it.
A fellowship so rich that it brings total trust.
I want that!
I want it for me and those I love.
I want it for Addison.
Lord, may it be so!

"The Turtle and the Hair...y Dog"

I *LOVE* Surprises!
So...when the Lord, sent me a special birthday surprise...
On my 61st birthday,
I was very excited!
I had not seen a turtle "in the wild"...within reach...
Since I was a little girl...a long time ago!!

Our dog, Wally, alerted me to the turtle's presence, with his barking.
I looked out the window and grabbed my camera.
I started thanking the Lord for such a nice surprise...
Wondering if God was telling me something.

I observed the turtle as he sauntered through our yard...
Waddling within inches of Wally's nose.
Wally barked and strained on his leash...
Trying to reach the turtle.
I am not sure what his plan was, but he *WANTED* that turtle!!
I was not concerned, for the dog was on a leash...under my control!

I suddenly thought of Satan's ploys.
1 Peter 5, verses 8 and 9 *(NIV)* tell us...
*"Be self- controlled and alert.
Your enemy the devil prowls around like a roaring lion
Looking for someone to devour.
Resist him, standing firm in the faith..."*

Satan can do nothing unless God allows it.
We, however, are to be self-controlled and alert.
We cannot "play" with sin...
We cannot get too close.
Satan is on the prowl.
His plan is to deceive, devour, and destroy me.
I must resist and stand firm!

There are times, in Scripture, when God exhorts us…
Not to fight…but to flee!
We are to flee…
From sexual immorality, from idolatry, from youthful lusts…
Read 1 Corinthians 10:14 and 2 Timothy 2:22.
Don't play with sin! Run from sin!

Do you hear the enemy roaring?
Do you know he is straining on the leash?
Do you realize he would like to destroy you?

STAY AWAY FROM HIM!!
If a helpless turtle in a shell can resist his enemy...
We, with God's strength and armor, can surely resist the enemy of our soul!

"Waterlogged"

*"I lift up my eyes to the hills-
Where does my help come from?
My help comes from the Lord,
The Maker of heaven and earth."
(Psalm 121: 1 and 2, NIV)*

How often have I looked to the Lord for my help?
Many, many, many times...daily.
He is my life.
He is my source.

Psalm 3, verses 3 and 4 *(NKJV)* say,
*"But you, O Lord, are a shield for me,
My glory and the One who lifts up my head.
I cried to the Lord with my voice,
And He heard me from His holy hill..."*

He lifts up my head...so I can lift up my eyes to Him.
But...where is my heart?
Am I crying to Him…
Or am I merely crying?

Sometimes my prayers become "waterlogged"!
Waterlogged...saturated...permeated...full.
Full of what?
Full of MY thoughts…MY worries…MY answers…
Full of ME.

Example:
My friend, "Jane", is taking a trip.
She has asked me to pray for safety and no car problems.

If I am truly looking to the Lord for help,
My prayer may sound something like this:
"Lord, You are the God who is everywhere…

I am trusting you to look over Jane.
Keep her safe in her travels, Lord.
You are her all powerful God.
Keep her car free from any problems, Lord.
I thank you for your care over my friend."

On the other hand, I can easily get "waterlogged".
Instead of being a prayer "warrior"...
I become a prayer "worrier".
My words may be the same...
But my underlying thoughts start to saturate my mind.
My heart stops looking to the Lord.
Instead, it becomes immersed in my own worries:
"Lord, please take care of Jane...
Keep her safe as she travels…"
(Ok...here come my own thoughts and worries...)
Take care of her in that old rickety car of hers...
I don't know why she keeps that old thing...
It's not like she can't afford something better...
I just know it's gonna lose its engine on this trip...
Then...what will she do?
Yep...she will call us...
And we will go help her, for sure...
But, we can't afford to take the time off...
And what if she calls on Tuesday?
We can't go on Tuesday...
We already have plans...dinner with Sue and Tom...
Hmmm...I wonder what I should make.
Oh dear...I think Sue is allergic to something...
What is that food she is allergic to?
Hmmm...I'd better call her."

And so...my prayers become waterlogged.
I become waterlogged.
My time with the Lord has become saturated with ME.
My prayer has become only a waterlogged "reflection".
Instead of looking *UP* to the hills...
I am looking *DOWN*...
And drowning in my worries.
Instead of focusing on the grandeur of the Lord...
I can see only the waterlogged reflection of the hills...
I have not left my burden with the Lord.
I have held onto it...
My thoughts have bogged me down...
As water bogs down floating leaves.

So what can I do?
How can I become a prayer warrior?
How can I overcome my tendency to be a prayer "worrier"?

To be a "warrior"...
I must put on the armor of God.

Read Ephesians 6: 10-20.
After listing the pieces of "spiritual armor", we need,
Paul says, in verse 18:
"With all prayer and petition,
Pray at all times in the Spirit,
And with this in view,
BE ON THE ALERT,
With all perseverance and petition for all the saints."

2 Corinthians 10:5 also speaks of the "weapons of our warfare".
We are to take *"every thought captive*
To the obedience of Christ."

When I notice my mind wandering during prayer...
I must re-focus.
I must be on the alert!
I must bring every thought captive to Christ.
I must look to Him...even to be able to pray.
I must admit, *"Lord I can't even pray...help me."*
He will "lift up my head",
So I can "lift up my eyes".
Then...I can focus on Him...
My eyes can meet His...
I can give Him the "undivided attention" He deserves.

As I *"lift up my eyes to the hills"*...
My help will come from Him.
I will fellowship with Him…and He with me.
I will give Him my burdens...
He will take those burdens upon Himself.

When my focus has been on Him…
I rise from prayer,
Knowing I have been with God...
Not "waterlogged"…
Not "weary"...
Not immersed in my "worries"...
But refreshed...
Restored...
At rest...
Knowing He has heard me from His holy hill...
Knowing I have been to His throne of grace...
Knowing I have communed with the "Maker of heaven and earth".

"Thou will keep him in perfect peace,
WHOSE MIND IS STAYED ON THEE:
Because he trusteth in thee."
Isaiah 26:3 (KJV)

"HANG ON!!"

Poor Cinnamon...
She was the epitome of the "scaredy cat".
She was hanging onto Mary for dear life!
Her nails were firmly embedded into Mary's shirt.
At first she just dangled there, unaware that Mary's arms were beneath her.
Then, Mary gently pulled her to safety.

I tell Mary that God has given her a special gift...
Animals seem to trust her.
Cinnamon was a kitten who ran from everyone...
Mary, however, scooped her up and held her.
Cinnamon retained some of her fear...
But Mary's care helped relieve those fears.

How do *WE* handle our fears?
God cares for us.
He understands us.
Do we trust *HIM?*
Do we let Him hold us...even if we are afraid??

God's Word tells us how to handle fear.
Isaiah 41:10 says:
"Do not fear, for I am with you."
And, in Psalm 56:4:

"...In God I have put my trust;
I shall not be afraid."

What should we do when our feelings of fear are seemingly unavoidable?
God understands our weaknesses.
Psalm 56:3 says…
"When I AM afraid, I will put my trust in you."

Keep trusting *HIM*.
Trust Him until your feelings catch up with your faith, and your fears are left behind you.
Know that He will not let you fall.
You may feel as though you are hanging on by your fingernails.
That is ok...
"Hang on!"
"Hang on tightly to Jesus!"
You may not see...but you can know...
"Underneath are the everlasting arms of God."

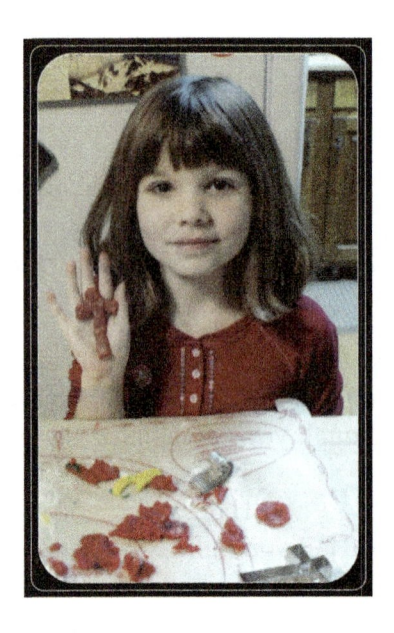

"I PRESENT TO YOU..."

Ella and I were cutting out cookies.
I wanted a picture of her.
As I prepared, she picked up the cross cut-out.
She held it up, and I focused my lens!
Grandma's heart was happy.
Of all the cookies Ella could have chosen...
She presented the cross.

Our family has seen more than the usual amount of trials lately.
Financial stresses.
Disappointments.
Deaths of family members and friends.
Illnesses.

Recently, our daughter suddenly became seriously ill.
A Saturday trip to Urgent Care resulted in questions, rather than answers.
A Monday ambulance drive to the Emergency Room,
After a fainting episode, still gave no concrete answer.
A Thursday doctor's visit with more blood work,
Finally gave a diagnosis of mononucleosis.
As difficult of a diagnosis that was...
It was a relief!

During those days,
God graced me with the quiet strength to control my thoughts.
I would not let my mind travel into my imaginations.
I waited, knowing God had it all under control.
I knew He cared.
I knew...because of the Cross.

We face many trials in this lifetime.
Disappointments, discouragement, betrayals, broken hearts.
What do we do when we travel through heartache?
What do we do when we wonder, "Does God care?"

We must do, in our spirits, the same thing Ella did.
We must lift up the cross.

When you are faced with the mockery of others,
When bullies pour out their contempt,
When the crowd seems to be plotting against you,
You ask, "Does God understand?"

Remember that Jesus was mocked and bullied.
The crowd that had once welcomed Him,
Turned and shouted, *"Crucify Him!"*
You wonder, "Does Jesus really understand?"
You ask, "Does God really care?"
Of course, He does!
What do I offer as proof?
I present to you...*THE CROSS!*

When you are faced with false accusations;
Those who have claimed to be your friends have "disappeared";
Those who once vowed to always be there for you,
Have denied any relationship.
And you ask, "Does God understand?"
"Does He know how I feel?"

Remember Peter...and Judas!
Judas betrayed Jesus with a kiss!
Peter said to Jesus:
*"Even though all may fall away because of you,
I will never fall away." (Matt. 26:33)*
Just a few hours later,
Peter began to curse and swear,
"I do not know the man!" (26:74)
You ask, "Does God understand? Does *HE* care?"
Of course He does!!
I present to you...*THE CROSS!*

How about when you are so weak you can barely stand!
You are physically, or emotionally, or mentally ill.
You are agonizing.
And you ask, "Does Jesus understand my weakness?"

Look at the Garden of Gethsemane.
Our Savior said, *"My soul is deeply grieved, to the point of death." (26:38)*
Look at Jesus..."*being in agony He was praying very fervently;*

And His sweat became as drops of blood, falling down upon the ground." (Luke 22:44)
You ask, "Does Jesus understand? Does God care?"
I know He cares!
I present to you...*THE CROSS!*

Mocked, falsely accused, betrayed, grieving!
Does Jesus understand?

Have you ever been condemned and forsaken?
Your soul is in darkness. You feel totally alone.
And you question God.
And you ask, "Why, God? Why?"
He feels so far away. Hope eludes you.

Does Jesus understand?
Look at *HIM*! Hear *HIM* as He cries out,
"MY GOD, MY GOD, WHY HAVE YOU FORSAKEN ME?" (Matt. 27:46)
Does Jesus care?
I present to you...*THE CROSS!*

I have to catch my breath as I contemplate the agony.
I am in awe as I look at Jesus on that cross.
Does He care???
Oh my...How could I ever doubt His love?
From the depths of His being...He cares!
As God the Son hung on that wooden cross,
God the Father had to turn his back.
You see...our sin was placed on Jesus.
God is holy...He turned away from that sin.

And we still wonder, Does God care?"
Does He really love me?
Oh my YES.
"But God demonstrates His own love toward us,
In that while we were yet sinners,
Christ died for us."
(Romans 5:8)
I present to you...*THE CROSS!*

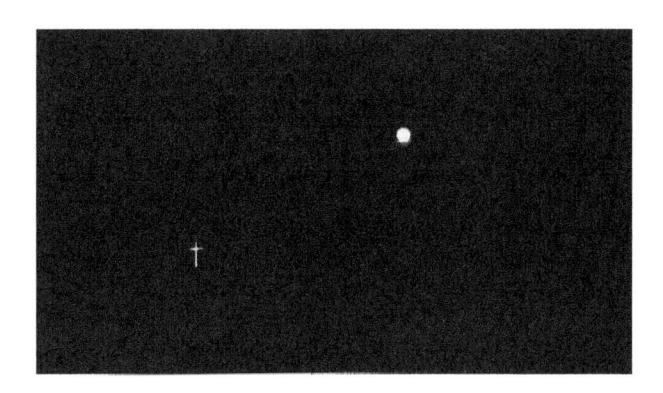

LOOK AND LIVE

The "Super Moon"!!!
Would the sky be clear or cloudy?
Would we be able to see the moon in all its glory?
Scientists said it could appear 30% brighter and 14% larger than the average full moon.
However, realistically, the difference, from such a distance,
Would be fairly difficult to notice.

It was suggested that some of the discussion about how amazing the moon appeared
Was actually due to the fact that not many people
Take the time
To look up at the moon.

My hubby and I took a short ride to see the "Super Moon".
We stopped...directly across from our church.
The contrast between the moon and the lighted cross struck me.
From our perspective...they were of comparable size.
And both were beautiful!

As I contemplated the remarks about the moon's splendor that evening,
I couldn't help but relate those thoughts to the Christ of the Cross.
He is always there,
But, not many people take the time
To look up at Him.

The Cross is amazing.
Christ is amazing.
People hear…they acknowledge.
But few…take the time…to look up.
And…it is only
The look of faith…that saves.

Jesus said, in John 3: 14 and 15:
"As Moses lifted up the serpent in the wilderness,
Even so must the Son of Man be lifted up;
So that whoever believes will in Him
Have eternal life."

Jesus was referring to a time in the Old Testament.
The people had sinned.
Poisonous snakes were surrounding them.
Snake bites were killing them.
God instructed Moses to place a brazen snake on a pole and lift it up.
Victims of the snake bite were instructed to look up at that brazen serpent.
Whoever looked...lived!

Jesus was lifted up on the Cross.
He died to pay for the "snakebite" of sin we all have.
How are we saved from our sin?
Look up.
Look to the Cross! Look to Christ!
Believe!

In John 6: 40 *(NIV)*, Jesus says,
"For my Father's will is
That everyone who looks to the Son
And believes in Him,
Shall have eternal life..."

Faith is... the eyes of the soul...gazing upon the cross...
Seeing Jesus, the Son of God, dying to pay for my sin,
And believing in Him.
Knowing He alone is my way to Heaven,
I place all my trust in Him!

Take the time...to look up...*NOW!*
Believe!
Look and Live!!

COMFORT

TO MELT

THE DESPAIRING HEART

"CLOUD COVER"

The Snow Storm had subsided.
As I gazed out the window, I noticed the sun was shining.
Its brightness, however, was dulled.
Cloud cover hovered between me and the sun's exuberance.
The sun was aglow, as always.
My vision, however, was blurred by the clouds.
I could not feel the warmth of the sun.
I could only feel the chill of the storm.

Today, a few days later, I again look out my window.
The cloud cover has dissipated.
The sun is brightly illuminating the sky.
Its brilliance is magnificent.
Its warmth has returned.

Sometimes, snow storms fall into our souls.
We don't invite them.
A blizzard hits us fiercely.
Cold winds howl through us.
Even when the storm subsides, we are left with its effects.
Clouds continue to blur our vision.
God seems far away, even though we know He is always near.
Our sense of His presence seems dulled.
Our souls struggle to feel the warmth of the Son.
The cloud cover is heavy.
We wait. We wonder.
We walk...by faith alone.
We cannot see, but we believe.
We trust the faithfulness of our God.

In December 1963, a storm struck our family.
My sweet six year old cousin died of leukemia.
I do not remember how long she had fought the disease.
In those days, effective treatment options were few.

The cloud cover lingered.

I could not imagine the deep pain and sorrow her mother endured.
I am sure that from the day of Debbie's diagnosis...
Until her death...and for days beyond...
My Aunt Arlene, Debbie's Mommy, grieved.
Waiting; wondering;
Trusting through the tears.

Forty nine years later, in December 2012,
Aunt Arlene entered Heaven!
I wonder...did God send Debbie to welcome her?
I can only imagine the scene...the joy!
What jubilation! What contentment! What overwhelming peace!!
The final and fulfilling and forever reunion!
Any "cloud cover" left from earthly sorrow evaporated.
All grief was immediately erased.
The days when my aunt had longed to hold Debbie just once more?
They were forever finished!
The questions? Satisfied!
The years of separation? Gone!
The earthly trials no longer mattered.
They were a faint speck…
Not worth a consideration in this present glory!
In comparison to Heaven's happiness, they were insignificant!
Aunt Arlene and her beloved daughter were together!
Together...with their Savior... forever and ever and ever...for eternity!

The years on this earth, whether many or few,
Are only as a few grains of sand on the seashores of eternity.
Know that God is faithful and just!
He will make all things right!!

Eternity in our eternal Home will be magnificent!
It will be worth the wait!
Revelation 22:3-5 give us a peek through the "window"!

"There will no longer be any curse;
And the throne of God and of the Lamb will be in it,
And His bond- servants will serve Him.
THEY WILL SEE HIS FACE,
And His name will be on their foreheads.
And there will no longer be any night;
And they will not have need of the light of a lamp nor the light of the sun,
Because the Lord God will illumine them;
And they will reign forever and ever."

Someday, all cloud cover will vanish!
There will be nothing to block the Brightness of the Son!
We will see Him clearly, in all His glory!

The warmth of His Presence will not be hindered.
We will see Him "face to face".

"TRAIN TRACKS AND TRIALS"

Do you see the train approaching?
It is so far in the distance that it is yet unseen!
When will it arrive?

We live in a town with a railroad crossing at its hub!
When the train whistle sounds in the distance...
When the railroad gate lowers,
Approaching cars sit and wait...and drivers wonder...

"Which train is coming?"
Is it the speedy and short Amtrak train?
Or must we wait for the long, slow, one hundred car freight train?

Trials are much like trains.
We are not always aware that one is approaching.
We may hear the sound in the distance...
A door slamming shut;
A phone ringing during the night;
A siren wailing.
Life changes in an instant.

Some of our trials are short and pass quickly.
Others are long and chronic and threaten to plunge us into despair.

How can we handle trials and tribulations??
We cannot "outrun" a train.
We can only run to a safe place.

My safe place is Jesus.
He is my steady Rock.
I run to Him.

What does He offer me??

He offers me wisdom during my trials.
"But if any of you lacks wisdom, let him ask of God,
Who gives to all generously and without reproach,
And it will be given to him." (James 1:5)

He offers me comfort.
"Blessed be the God and Father of our Lord Jesus Christ,
The Father of mercies and God of all comfort,
Who comforts us in all our affliction
So that we will be able to comfort those who are in any affliction
With the comfort with which we ourselves are comforted by God."
2 Corinthians 1: 3 and 4

He offers me peace.
"Peace I leave with you; My peace I give to you;
Not as the world gives do I give to you.
Do not let your heart be troubled, nor let it be fearful."
John 14:27

He offers me His presence.
"For He Himself has said,
'I will never leave you nor forsake you.' "
Hebrews 13:5 (NKJV)

Jesus offers you all you need.
RUN TO HIM!!

"PLANTED ON THE ROCK"

Whenever my Dad was at our home during the winter,
He enjoyed taking responsibility for keeping our deck shoveled.
After one of our last snowfalls,
He said to me, "I think I'll go shovel the deck."

I responded, "Be careful.
There may be some slippery spots."

He answered me with a smirk,
"My head gets mixed up, but my feet are still in good shape."
Then, he laughed.

Dad's last year on earth was very difficult for him.
Within a matter of months,
He lost his license and his car.
Without them, he was unable to take his almost daily trips to enjoy meals with friends.
He moved out of his home of thirty six years.
His beloved sister, Arlene, moved on to Heaven.
His home was sold.

We did our best to keep him happy.
But, he was often overwhelmed with all the loss.
The day God took him Home was bittersweet for us.
Difficult...because we love and miss him.
Sweet...because his sadness is over.

Dad accepted Christ as his Savior when he was just a child.
Throughout his life, he served in his church.
In later years, he became a Gideon and gave out God's Word to many people.
He always carried a Gideon New Testament in his shirt pocket.

During good times, and bad, his feet were planted on the Rock!

Most of us are familiar with Jesus' story of the wise and foolish men.
Matthew 7: 24-27 records the story:
"Therefore, everyone who hears these words of Mine, and acts on them,
May be compared to a wise man who built his house on the rock.
And the rain fell, and the floods came, and the winds blew and slammed against that house;
And yet it did not fall, for it had been founded on the rock.
Everyone who hears these words of Mine and does not act on them,
Will be like a foolish man who built his house on the sand.
The rain fell, and the floods came, and the winds blew and slammed against that house;
And it fell–and great was its fall."

Are your feet planted on the Rock?

Psalm 61:2 *(KJV)* says,
"From the end of the earth will I cry unto thee,
When my heart is overwhelmed:
Lead me to the rock that is higher than I."

There are times in this life, when our hearts are overwhelmed.
My Dad experienced those times, as we all do.
But...his feet were planted on the Rock.

About a month before the Lord took Dad Home...
I was walking past my Dad's bedroom.
It was very early in the morning.

I heard him speaking, and realized he was talking to the Lord.
It was a prayer that touched my heart.
And it showed the heart that my Dad had for the Lord
The following was his prayer:

"When we all get to Heaven, what a day that will be.
What a day that will be.
When we all get to Heaven, what a day that will be, Lord.
Thank you for being with me all the days of my life…the good, and the bad.
Lord…help me never forget what You did for me.
Help me to honor You the rest of my life."

Dad's feet were planted on the Rock.
And now, he is *WITH* the Rock of his salvation.
The burdens of this life are forever lifted. He is free!

Are YOUR feet planted on the ROCK?

"DARKNESS"

Does life hurt?
Yes, often, it does.
Sometimes, we give thanks, not because of our obvious blessings.
We give thanks...just because!

The Old Testament book of Habakkuk is a favorite of mine!
Habakkuk was disturbed because of the sin that was rampant in his nation.
He questioned God, basically asking, "Why don't you do something?"
God's answer? He *WAS* doing something...behind the scenes.
He was going to use the wicked empire of Babylon
To defeat and bring judgment on Judah.

This discovery left Habakkuk with even more questions!
How could God do such a thing?
The dialogue continued.

Ultimately, what is the answer to all our "whys"?
The answer is "Who"!
HE IS GOD!

Habakkuk 2:4 is an "anchor" verse.
It is repeated in Romans and in Galatians,
"...The righteous will live by his faith."
Even in "hopeless" times...God's people have hope.
Those who know Him, live by faith.

Habakkuk's final conclusion?
*"Though the fig tree should not blossom
And there be no fruit on the vines,*

Though the yield of the olive should fail
And the fields produce no food,
Though the flock should be cut off from the fold
And there be no cattle in the stalls,
YET I WILL EXULT IN THE LORD,
I WILL REJOICE IN THE GOD OF MY SALVATION.
THE LORD GOD IS MY STRENGTH,
And He has made my feet like hinds' feet,
And makes me walk on my high places." (3:17-19)

Habakkuk knew that difficult times were approaching.
Yet, in spite of the darkness he was experiencing,
He praised the Lord anyway!
He was thankful...not because of what he had.
He was thankful...just because.
He was thankful because God was, and would remain...
Even in perilous times...
Habakkuk's salvation and strength!

Are you walking through difficult times?
Is your family walking through difficult times?
Is your nation walking through difficult times?

Are you questioning God?
Does He seem far away?
Are you experiencing darkness within your heart?
Is despair knocking at your door?

Talk to God.
Wait for His answer.
Do not let feelings of discouragement rule you!

God is at work...behind the scenes!
He is your strength and salvation.
Be thankful...just because!
He is worthy of our praise.
He will make all things right!
HE IS GOD!

"DOES JESUS CARE?"

Early morning…
The sun had not yet peeped over the horizon.
The restfulness of sleep had evaded me.
I was sitting on the couch…
Speaking only to God…

My heart was hurting.
Was there one who knew?
Was there one who understood?
Was there one who cared?

Then…I heard it!
I knew immediately what it was.
Although it was still dark outside…
The simple song of a single bird.
And I knew what God was saying…
For I had read it in his Word.

"Look at the birds of the air,
That they do not sow, nor reap nor gather into barns,
And yet your heavenly Father feeds them.
Are you not worth much more than they?" (Matthew 6:26)

Peace entered my heart.
The circumstances had not changed.
But I had changed.
I was reminded that, indeed, God did care.

Luke 12:6 reveals a similar sentiment.
"Are not five sparrows sold for two cents?
Yet not one of them is forgotten before God.
Indeed, the very hairs of your head are all numbered.
Do not fear;
You are more valuable than many sparrows."

It is amazing to me that God cares for the birds as He does.
They seem so small; so "insignificant".
Indeed, they are small.
Can you see them in the picture above?
Tiny, tiny creatures in a huge, huge world.
God has created a vast world.
Yet…He cares for every living being…every little bird…each one!

In the early 1800's, Frank Graeff was known as the "sunshine minister",
Because of his cheerful and winsome personality.
Few knew of the many severe testing experiences in Mr. Graeff's life.
During a time of great despondency, doubt, and physical pain,
He turned to God's Word.
First Peter 5:7 *(KJV)* gave him the comfort and assurance he needed.
"Casting all your care upon Him, for He careth for you."
After meditating on that truth,
Graeff wrote the lyrics to the beloved hymn, "Does Jesus Care?"

Decades ago, a motorcycle accident claimed the life of one of my cousins.
There were many grief stricken friends and relatives at that funeral.
I had no doubt that the ones who hurt the most deeply were his loving parents.
The hymn they chose to be sung at the funeral was, "Does Jesus Care?"
It left a lasting impression on me.
I will close with two of the verses and the chorus.

"Does Jesus care when my heart is pained
Too deeply for mirth or song.
As the burdens press, and the cares distress
And the way grows weary and long?

Does Jesus care when I've said good bye
To the dearest on earth to me
And my sad heart aches till it nearly breaks,
Is it aught to Him? Does He see?

Oh yes, He cares, I know He cares.
His heart is touched with my grief;
When the days are weary, the long nights dreary,
I know my Savior cares."

"LOOK BEYOND"

As a child, I was terrified of the darkness.
I often stayed with my grandparents, who lived in a big old farm house.
Their country home was surrounded by large trees.
Even the light from the moon did not always reach the windows.

My grandfather, a farmer, often arose in the pre-dawn darkness.
In order to plug in his coffee pot, he had to unplug the light that shone into my room.
Without fail, I awoke as soon as the room went dark.
As soon as I opened my eyes, I would start screaming.
My grandma would yell down the steps,
"Jimmy, turn that light back on!"
The lamp would immediately come back on.
The light would swallow up the darkness.
I would go back to sleep.
I do not know how many mornings my poor Grandpa went without his coffee.
(And I wondered why he was so often in a bad mood.)

Darkness invades our lives.
As a child, I discovered how I could walk dark pathways.
If I was walking on the path from the barn to the house,
I looked beyond the darkness.
I could focus on the house's porch light.
As I got closer, the darkness lost its terror.
Soon, I had reached the entrance.
The door opened.

The light flooded the room.
I was safely home.

Darkness invades our souls.
It is often accompanied by fear...even terror.
How can we walk through these dark nights of the soul?

Our church is located across from a cemetery.
I have often walked through that cemetery.
Reading epitaphs...pondering.
Not too long ago, I discovered an encouraging image.
The cross on the front of our little church can be easily seen...
Beyond the array of headstones.

Death can be a terrifying thing.
The darkness can overwhelm us.
Is it possible to look beyond the gravestones?
Is it possible to walk through this dark valley of death and overcome the fear?
Is it possible to find hope after the death of a loved one?
Is it possible to live without fearing death?

It is possible...
If we can look beyond the darkness...
Even if we must look through our tears...
If we can look beyond the experience of dying...
If we can look beyond our pain and suffering...
If we can look beyond the grave...
And see the cross.

"God demonstrates His own love toward us,
In that while we were yet sinners,
Christ died for us." (Romans 5:8)
God reached down to us.
He proved He loves.
He proved He cares.

"For God so loved the world" (you and me)
"That He gave His only begotten Son," (Jesus)...
"That whoever" (that's you and me)
"Believes in Him" (Jesus)...
"Shall not perish," (die forever)...
"But have eternal life." (now and forever)
(John 3:16)

Do you believe?
Jesus said, *"...Everyone who looks to the Son*
And believes in Him
Shall have eternal life..." (John 6:40 NIV)

In your heart, look at the Cross.

Look at Jesus…
Dying for you...
Your sin...on His shoulders...
Tell Him..."Lord, I believe.
Thank you for dying for me.
I trust in You to give me eternal life."

He will give you life.
When darkness comes...
And, in this life, it will...
Look beyond the darkness...
Look at the cross.
Look to Jesus.

Think of His sacrifice...
Let your heart be drawn to the empty tomb...
Know that He is alive.
He will be with you when you have to travel dark paths.
He will hold your hand.
And if, one day, you find yourself in the valley of the shadow of death...
He will be with you there, as well.
He will give you the strength to look beyond the darkness...
He will help you focus on the "porch light" of Heaven.
As you approach the entrance, the gate will open.
The light of the Son will flood your soul.
You will be safely home.

CONSTANCY

TO MELT

THE DEDICATED HEART

"A LEGACY OF FAITH"

"For the Lord is good;
His lovingkindness is everlasting
And His faithfulness to all generations."
(Psalm 100:5)

My Dad was born in 1922.
His great granddaughter, pictured with him in the above picture,
Entered our family in 2006.
She absolutely adored her "Pa"!

Dad entered Heaven in April 2014, at the age of ninety-one
He had twelve grandchildren, twenty-seven great grandchildren,
And a great great grandchild due in October.
I remember once, when the whole family was together,
My Mom looked at my Dad during all the commotion.
She exclaimed, "We started all this!"

Dad was raised on the "Canary farm",
The Canarys were a close knit family.
They loved each other.
And they loved and served the Lord.

Each of the seven brothers and sisters
Married and raised children.
These children then married and raised children,
Who married and are raising children.

There is nothing terribly unique about that scenario.
It has continued on since the creation of Adam and Eve.
The Bible gives a variety of lists on who "begat" who...
Down through the generations.

The truth for which I am thankful is the legacy of it all...
Legacy...what is left behind for the next generation.
Pericles said, *"What you leave behind*
Is not what is engraved in stone monuments…
But what is woven into the lives of others."

Granted, true faith is not "handed down".
There comes that moment in each life...
That "day" of decision…
Will I put my trust in Christ and follow Him...
Or not?
Regardless of the parents' influence or lack thereof.
Each of us must make that choice.

On the other hand, parents can set the foundation.
They can guide...
Through words...
Through actions...
Through attitudes.

Anne Graham Lotz, daughter of Billy and Ruth Graham,
Said of her mother,
"It was her love for the Lord Jesus, with whom she walks every day,
That made me want to love Him
And walk with Him like that."

I am thankful for the "legacy of faith"
Woven into my life.
As children, we attended church every Sunday.
I can still remember the pew in which we sat.
I can still see my Dad, hymnbook in hand, singing the old hymns.

I recall some of the stories my Dad told me…
Recollections of the part he had, as a teenager,
In the building of a Christian camp...
Sacandaga Bible Conference!

I remember listening to my Dad discuss
The death of Jesus with a "church leader",
Who thought it would have been just fine if Jesus had not shed His blood for us.
My Dad explained to this person the Bible basics...
"…Without shedding of blood there is no forgiveness" (Hebrews 9:22)

My parents ran a dairy farm.
They were very busy...and often tired.

But my Dad read the paper each day.
We watched "Bonanza" on Sunday nights.
And...Sunday was the Lord's Day...
The cows got milked...but other chores were limited.
We went to church...
Whether it was haying season or not...
Rain, snow, or sunshine...
We went to church!

My Dad was also a fan of Billy Graham!
Etched in my memory is seeing Dad,
One autumn evening in 1963,
Walk into the living room, turn on the TV,
And then head back out to the kitchen,
Where he could read the paper, but still see the TV.
He could not have known that, on that evening,
As I sat in that living room chair,
The Lord would reveal Himself to me.
I would understand the gospel.
I would accept Christ as my Savior!

My Dad served the Lord.
In addition to his service in his church,
He was a "Gideon".
He passed out New Testaments.
He kept one in his shirt pocket!
He witnessed to others about Jesus!

I am very thankful for my Dad...
He was a caring soul.
He had a giving heart.
He had a good sense of humor.
He loved his family.
He loved His Lord!
He "wove" a legacy of faith into my life!

Thank you, Dad!
Happy Father's Day in Heaven!
I wonder if you are spending "Father's Day" with *YOUR* father.
It must be so amazing to be forever in the presence of our *HEAVENLY FATHER!*
I love you!
I thank our Lord for you!
Thank you for the legacy of faith!

"STEERING THE STROLLER"

"Grandma, can I push CJ?"
Caroline reached up and grabbed the stroller handle.
With great confidence, she began wheeling her baby brother down the driveway.
Since she could not see over the top of the stroller...
She could not see the path ahead of them.
She was content just knowing that she was the "big sister"...
The big sister who loved her little brother and wanted to help guide him...
Guide him along a path she could not see.

Periodically, Grandma would reach over and take the handle with Caroline.
I would steer her in the right direction.
I would keep the stroller on the path.

As a parent and now a grandparent...
I have found myself in similar circumstances.
I have been content just knowing I was the "Mommy"...
The "Mommy" who loves her child and wants to guide her...
Guide her along a path...
A path I cannot see!

But I know the one who does see the path ahead of my child.
I look to *HIM!*
HE takes the handle!
HE steers me in the right direction!
HE keeps us on the path!

I have often relied on Proverbs 3, verses 5 and 6 *(KJV)*:
Trust in the Lord with all thine heart;
And lean not unto thine own understanding,
In all thy ways acknowledge Him,
And He shall direct thy paths."

All the knowledge a Mom or Dad may acquire...
Can never compare to the superior knowledge of our God.
The wisdom of this world, especially in "child rearing"...
Fluctuates with each generation of new "experts".
Nothing can replace the need for full trust in our God.

HE alone is fully trustworthy!
HE alone sees the path ahead of us!
HE alone can bring us to our appointed goal!

We must know God!
The word, "acknowledge", in the statement,
"In all thy ways acknowledge Him..."
Does not refer to a simple nod of recognition.
It infers an intimate knowledge of God!
Observe Him!
Get to know Him!
Study His Word...
Know His ways.

Parents have a joy...and a responsibility... of extreme magnitude.
At various times, grandparents, teachers, and other care-givers...
Are given the joy...and responsibility...of sharing that task.
So...we grip the handle of the stroller carrying our child...
And we walk along the path ahead of us.

The path is not always smooth!
At times, it is filled with irritating pebbles.
Other times, I have to steer around boulders.
Twists and turns surprise me.
Even when I can see a turn coming...
Rounding that turn may bring an unexpected challenge.

Steep hills are not easy to climb...
I would prefer the flat prairies.
Sometimes, I trip and fall on my knees.
I discover this place is a good place to be.
For, on my knees, I stop for a while.
I cry out to God:
"Lord, I can't do this...
You must take the handle...
You alone have the strength...
You alone have the wisdom!"

And...then...He lifts me up.
He gives me *HIS* strength.
He provides me with *HIS* wisdom.
I continue on the path...
But I am no longer leaning on myself...
I am resting in Him and learning His ways.
I am leaning on Him...He is my strong tower!
As I walk...His Word is in my hand...in my mind...in my heart.
I am getting to know *HIM!*
I can continue on this journey...
For *HE* is directing my path!

"FOLLOW ME"

Caroline loves her little red wagon.
Pulling it up and down the driveway is great fun.
Sometimes it is empty.
Other times, it holds rocks or acorns.

One day, Caroline, with her wagon in tow, was following Gramma.
I glanced behind me to make sure she was ok.
In that moment, I noticed *HOW* she was following me.

She wasn't just casually sauntering behind me.
She was actually and deliberately keeping in line with my path.
If I moved to the left, she moved to the left.
If I stayed in the center of the driveway for a while, so did she.
If I wandered to the right, she wandered to the right.
She was *REALLY* following me.....*CLOSELY.*

In the early days of Jesus' ministry, He began calling His disciples...
His followers.
Matthew 4:19 tells us how, as Jesus was walking by the Sea of Galilee,
He saw Simon who was called Peter,
And Andrew, his brother,
Casting a net into the sea;
For they were fishermen.

"And He said to them,
'Follow Me,
And I will make you fishers of men.' "

The Greek words translated "follow me" in verse 6, literally say,
"Come here after Me"
Jesus wanted His followers to follow Him closely.
They were to stay near Him, not just watch from a distance.

What kind of a follower of Christ am I?
Do I just follow from a distance, not getting too close?
Do I follow...only if He goes where I want Him to go?
Only if He doesn't veer off the path I have chosen?
Only if He lets me stop periodically to play with the "stuff"
I have accumulated in my "little red wagon" I pull behind me?

Oh, the lessons I can learn from a little child!!
"Lord, help me to follow You closely.
Give me the strength to focus on you.
I don't want to be just a casual observer.
I don't want to be one who follows you only from a distance.
I want to walk "right on your heels".
Following You...closely."

"KEEPING IN STEP"

Grandchildren are a reward!
They bring to our lives a special kind of love,
A special kind of joy, a special kind of responsibility.

The above image is of my hubby taking a walk with one of our granddaughters.
Caroline's Mommy was busy caring for her new baby.
Grandpa decided that he would entertain Caroline for a while.
I love the image of Caroline "keeping in step" with Grandpa!

Proverbs 17:6 tells us,
"Children's children are the crown of old men..." (KJV)
The crown: The reward.
I find it interesting that Psalm 103:4 uses the same "crown" symbol.
This Psalm praises and blesses the Lord...
"...Who crowneth thee with lovingkindness and tender mercies." (KJV)

I believe that our grandchildren are a gift from our Lord...
A gift that, once again, manifests some of God's qualities...
Loving kindness and tender mercies!

My husband and I *LOVE* being grandparents.
We are thankful for these gifts from the loving hand of God.
We are showered with a special kind of love.

James Dobson is the founder of *Focus on the Family*.
He once spoke of an essay a nine year old girl wrote.
The subject was, "What is a Grandmother?"
Some of her thoughts were amusing,
Such as, "Usually grandmothers are fat, but not too fat to tie your shoes."
The sentiment that Dobson particularly found intriguing?
The insight at the close of the essay:
"They are the only grown-ups who have time."

Time?
As "older" people without the constant and daily responsibilities...
Demands that come with parenting young children...
We can more easily set aside "time"...
Time for just being there when needed...
Time to tell stories...
Time to play...
Time to teach...
Time to comfort and understand...
Time to guide with the perspective of older people.
Time to make our grandchildren feel extra special.
Time to show a unique kind of unconditional love.

Grandparents are a library of information...
Connecting children to their past.
They are also a library of knowledge...
Gained through years of experiences...
Walking books filled with stories...
Stories of God's faithfulness throughout generations!

My grandchildren love to hear stories:
Stories about Mommy when she was little,
Stories about Grandma when she was young,
Stories about Marriages...
Stories about Births...
Stories about Jesus:
Stories about answered prayers...
A legacy of stories.

In Deuteronomy 4:9, God directs His people:
He wants them to remember...and pass along...
His saving acts...His promises.

"Only take heed to yourself, and diligently keep yourself,
Lest you forget the things your eyes have seen,
And lest they depart from your heart all the days of your life.
And teach them to your children and your grandchildren." (NKJV)

Parents and grandparents have a huge responsibility before God.
I liken it to the truth of Philippians 4:9, when Paul said,

"The things you have learned and received and heard and seen in me,
Practice these things, and the God of peace will be with you."
In essence, I believe Paul was saying...
"Keep in step with me...for I keep in step with Christ."

Are you keeping in step with Christ?
When your children and grandchildren walk with you...
Are they learning to walk with Christ?
When they "keep in step" with you...
Are they "keeping in step" with the Lord?

I don't know how you feel...
But I feel very unworthy.
I know that, apart from the mercy of Christ...
I will fail.

I stumble...
I fall...
I get "out of step".
I find myself on the wrong path.
I do not walk closely enough to Him
But...I have hope in Him...
I am unworthy, but He is merciful.

I do not deserve the grandchildren I have.
Just their presence is an example of God's loving kindness to me.
My prayer?
"Please, Lord, let these precious grandchildren know You.
Let them see You in me.
Help them see beyond my faults and inconsistencies.
When I stumble...let them see me get up and get back in step with You.
May they walk with You on steady ground.
May they not stumble over the stones the enemy would place in their way.
And, finally, may their walk with You be stronger than mine.
May they know You, love You, live for You.
And always, Lord, please...
May they keep in step... with You."

"STANDING ON THE WORD THAT STANDS"

God's Word is an amazing Book!
It is the Letter of the Lord to His people.
Somehow, we have lost the awe that should come with this Truth!
Our Creator has given us a *Book*!
Its pages are filled with the Wisdom of God.

Isaiah 40:8 tells us:
"The grass withers, the flower fades;
But the word of our God stands forever."

We live in a beautiful area of our country.
But, it is always changing…with the seasons.
Our two year old granddaughter looked out the window one day and said,
"Mommy, what's wrong with the trees?"
Autumn had arrived. The leaves were changing color!

1 Peter 1, verses 24 and 25, reiterate and expand on the verse in Isaiah:
"All flesh is as grass,
And all the glory of man as the flower of the grass.
The grass withers, and its flower falls away,
But the word of the Lord endures forever." (NKJV)

God's Word is not like a fading or falling flower!
It does not change as the seasons.
It does not wither.
It stands strong during the seasons of our lives.

Spring; summer; fall; winter…
Each season brings its own joys and its own challenges.

During the "spring" of my life…
God's Word became *real* to me.
1 Peter 1:23 tells us that we are *"born again…*
Through the living and enduring word of God."

I heard God's Word that Jesus was the Son of God.
He had died for my sins and had risen again.
I put my trust in Him and was born again.

It was also during this season of "spring"…
I made another life changing decision.
I began the habit of spending time in God's Word…each day.
God's Word became my "daily bread" for spiritual nourishment.
It provided me with strength and sustenance and guidance.

Then, the excitement and busyness and heat of summer arrived.
I was a young wife and mother.
Searching for direction and priorities.
With the voices of society calling from every direction,
The call of God's voice stood strong.
Titus 2:4, 5 assured me of the value God places on motherhood.
Young women are encouraged…
"…To love their husbands, to love their children…"
Read that passage…it will guide you.

But, my summer was not without dryness.
There were times when it seemed like the "rain" was being withheld.
Days of doubt; days of depression; days of despair.

Post-partum clinical depression drained hope from me.
Retaining anything from the Word seemed nearly impossible…
Like filling a wicker basket with water.
I hung onto every bit of Truth that would "Velcro" to my soul.
And slowly…but surely…His Word prevailed.
God's Word stood strong!

False accusations and deceit catapulted us into months of legal and financial strain.
But, thankfully, just hours before we were "plunged" into this trial,
I was reading the Word.
One verse seemed to "jump" off the page and into my soul.
God's message to me was:
"Men will take you where you do not want to go,
But you keep trusting Me."
We trusted Him.
God's Word stood strong!

Autumn has recently arrived.
In our area…and in my life.
My children are grown.
I have retired from the fulfilling job of teaching kindergarten.
During this season, in my eyes, the beauty of God's earth explodes!
The colors are deep and rich and intense.
My grandchildren have brought to me a new richness!
Each one has brought his/her own special color to my life!

God's Word continues to guide me.
I asked Him what else I could do to continue serving Him.
Into my mind, came the words,
"What is that in thine hand?" (Exodus 4:2, KJV)
I knew immediately.
I had just finished a photography course and had loved it!
God wanted me to use my camera to serve Him.

I am loving autumn!
It is a beautiful time.
My grandchildren have brought me a special kind of beauty.
I am enjoying taking pictures and sharing the Word with you.
God's Word continues to feed me with the "finest of wheat".
God's Word stands strong!

Unless the Lord comes, winter will arrive.
I am hoping it will be an "easy" winter;
I know it will be filled with its own kind of beauty.
I know it may bring cold days.
But, I know my Lord is faithful!

God's Word has sustained me through the years.
Receiving it as my daily bread has made all the difference.
Having it ready…in my heart and mind,
Has prepared me for the times I would unexpectedly need it.
God's Word has been there for me in the past.
It is there for me now…in the present.
It will be there for me in the future.

We can firmly plant our feet on the foundation of the Bible.
God's Word endures forever.
When the flowers fade,
And when the grass withers,
We can stand on the Word that stands.
God's Word will stand strong!

"WAITING AND WATCHING"

Caroline and Gramma *LOVE* to take walks together.
Whenever I walk past her house,
I anticipate seeing her little face at the window,
Or hearing her run to the front door, exclaiming,
In her sweet little "Caroline" voice…
"Gramma…Caroline take walk with you?
I get my flip flops on!"
She gets ready as quickly as she can,
Rushes out the door and down the steps,
Runs to give me a kiss and hug,
And we take our walk.

One morning, I received a text message from her Mommy,
"Are you taking a walk?"
My response was yes!
"Caroline is waiting at the window for you!"
I answered that it would be about a half hour.
I asked if she thought her daughter could be patient.
That query was met with a ha-ha!

About a half hour later,
Gramma was on her way to pick up Caroline.
I received the above photo message from Sarah.
It pulled at my soul strings.
It melted my "Gramma heart!"

Caroline…
All ready to go…
Watching with anticipation for Gramma to appear…
Eagerly and expectantly waiting!

Yes...she knew I was coming;
She was waiting for me...But more than that...
She was watching!
She was eagerly anticipating!

When I rounded the curve, I saw her, sitting on the step.
I yelled, "Caroline!!"
She bounded down the steps and ran to me.
I got my kiss and hug!
We had a wonderful walk together.

Philippians 3:20 says,
"...*We eagerly wait for a Savior,*
The Lord Jesus Christ."
"Eagerly wait" translates a Greek word that suggests
A deep longing and "tiptoe" anticipation!

Romans 8:19 *(KJV)* suggests that all of creation
Waits with *"earnest expectation"*...
A phrase which literally means,
"To watch with outstretched neck".

Are you all ready to go?
Are you watching with anticipation for the Lord to appear?
Are you eagerly and expectantly waiting?
Are you straining to see Him?

One day, the Lord will descend from Heaven with a shout!
His children will hear His voice!
We will go to be with Him!
"And so we shall always be with the Lord." I Thessalonians 4:17)

In Titus 2:12, 13, the Lord instructs us, His children,
"...*Live sensibly, righteously and godly in the present age,*
Looking for the blessed hope
And the appearing of the glory
Of our great God and Savior, Christ Jesus..."

Are you waiting passively?
Or...are the eyes of your soul set toward Him?
Are you watching?
Are you *looking* for him?
Are you stretching to see Him?

Sometimes, I gaze up into the deep blue sky.
Beautiful cloud formations cause me to wonder,
"Lord, are You coming?
Are You coming right *NOW?*"
I think, perhaps, if I continue gazing,
I will *SEE* Him!!
Wouldn't that be awesome??

There are times, when Caroline has been gone for a while...
She rushes into our home, looks up into my face,
And says, "Gramma, Caroline's here! I'm *BACK*!!"

I wonder what the Lord will say when he returns.
Perhaps, He will use similar words...
"My beloved children,
Whom I have loved before the foundation of the world,
Jesus is here!
I'M BACK!!!"

"THE KITE"

How long has it been since you have flown a kite?
Did you know that NASA encourages kite flying?
Such an activity teaches a child to recognize aerodynamic forces.
Imagine that! I thought it was just a "fun thing" to do on a breezy day!

Sometimes...I feel like a kite!
I am thankful for the excitement that comes with the flight.
But I am also thankful for the "control cord' (the official word for the "string").

The above picture was taken at a hot air balloon festival.
Kite flying is a popular pastime there, when the balloons are not in flight.
My grandson was in "control" of this particular kite!

Sometimes, I feel like a kite...
Waiting for the "aerodynamic forces" to lift me up.
Trying to be patient...
Swaying back and forth
Searching for the right path.
My consolation?
I have given the "control cord" to the Lord!

I feel like a kite…
Sometimes soaring...
Sometimes falling...
But God holds the string.

The wind blows…
Soft or strong...
But God holds the string.

The gentle breeze moves quietly sometimes.
At other times the harsh wind howls viciously...
But God holds the string.

At times, I fly free.
Occasionally, I become tangled...
But God holds the string.

Sometimes I see His hand...
Sometimes I do not...
But I trust His heart...
For *HE* holds the string.

Perhaps I feel I would be able to soar higher if He would just...let go.
But He knows that I would just get lost...
So He continues His hold on me.

He has promised to never leave me...
To never forsake me...
He will always hold me tightly.
He will not lose His grip on His child.
He holds the string!

"But as for me,
I trust in You, O Lord.
I say, 'You are my God.'
My times are in Your hand..."
(Psalm 31: 14, 15)

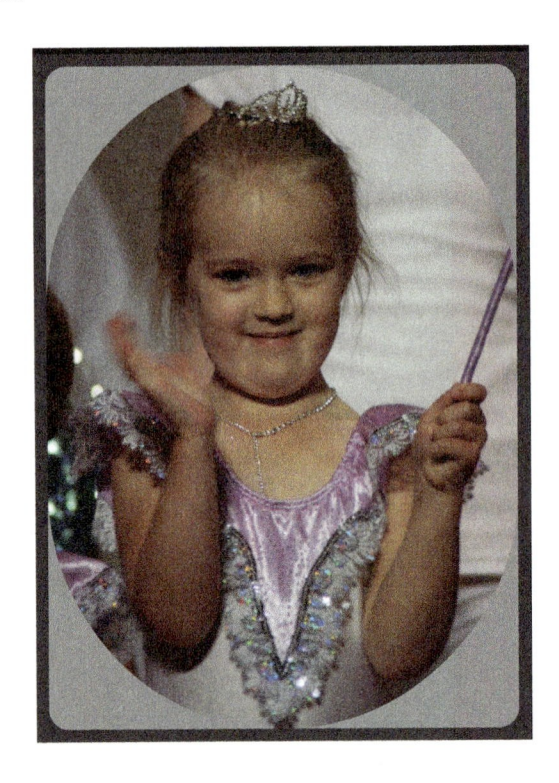

"HI GRANDMA"

Dress Rehearsal!!
Caroline was very excited!!
She looked gorgeous!
She was ready for action!

The group of "ballerina beauties" danced out onto the stage.
I had seated myself in the front row...good view; great pictures!
Caroline stopped in stage center and looked out into the audience.
In that second, she saw Grandma!
Without missing a beat of her dance,
She smiled and waved!
And, in that instant, Grandma's heart beat with joy!
In all the commotion of the moment, with all the responsibilities,
Caroline had acknowledged her Grandma.

Acknowledging the Lord is not merely a nod of recognition.
It involves all of the heart, observing and trusting Him.
It is an intimate knowledge of God.
It is a desire to have *HIM* in *ALL* my ways.

Psalm 91 speaks of God's care of His children.
Listen to verses 14 through 16 *(NIV)*.
'"Because he loves me,' says the Lord, 'I will rescue him;
I will protect him, for he acknowledges my name.
He will call upon me, and I will answer him.
I will be with him in trouble.

I will deliver him and honor him.
With long life will I satisfy him and show him my salvation.'"

A few days after dress rehearsal...
Caroline was sitting with me as I worked on the computer.
I showed her the picture, and I asked her,
"Who are you waving at?"

"I'm waving at you," she quickly responded.

"Why are you waving at me?" I queried.

"Because I love you," she said matter-of-factly!

There went my heart...again.

This "dress rehearsal" called life is full of responsibilities.
It is wrought with commotion!
But...at any time...I can look up and see Jesus "in the front row".
He is watching me!

I acknowledge *HIM*!
Why do I acknowledge the Lord?
Because I love Him!
I love Him with all my heart.
And...I hope... in that moment...I bring Him joy!

"THE EYES"

Meet our first *GREAT* grandson!!!
Wow...what a privilege!
God is certainly faithful to all generations!

Ethan III has amazing eyes!
His stares from those huge sparkly eyes can be mesmerizing!
But...I love this photo...
Not *ONLY* because of Little Ethan's eyes…
But because of His Daddy's eyes...
I can't see them...they are focused on his baby!
And, with the focus of his eyes, I see his smile...a grin of pure love and pride!

I have no doubt that my grandson, Ethan, will instruct and teach his son.
His love for his baby is unconditional.
I'm sure that there will be times that Ethan will guide him with "just a look"!
And Little Ethan, because he will know and love his Daddy...
Will know exactly what that look means!

God has *HIS* eyes on *HIS* children!
Psalm 33:18 promises that,
Behold, the eye of the Lord is on those who fear Him,
On those who hope for His lovingkindness."
He keeps His eyes on us...He loves us!

God also guides and counsels us with His eye!
"I will instruct you and teach you in the way which you should go;
I will counsel you with my eye upon you." (Psalm 32:8)

Do we know and love our Heavenly Daddy in such a way that...
We know what His "look" means?

God is watching us!
He may be watching with an eye of instruction.
He may be directing with an eye of discipline.
He may be teaching or counseling.
But He always looks with love!
Again...Do we know Him well enough to know what His "look" means?
Have we listened to and studied His Word enough to be able to recognize His voice?
Can we discern good and evil because we know His truth and practice it? (Hebrews 5:14)

Someday...we will see our Lord face to face.
When He looks at me...
I hope He smiles upon me.
I hope I hear Him say,
"Well done, good and faithful servant."
(Matthew 25:23, KJV)

"THE DREAM I NEVER HAD"

"Grandma, do you know the songs we sing at our church?"
Caroline brought out the hymnal.

"Well, I'm sure I know most of them," I responded.

"I want to find one you don't know and teach it to you."

So, we began the search.
After examining a dozen hymns, we found one.
She sang it for me.
I sang it with her.

Then, it was my turn.
"Do you know this one? How about that one?"
Finally, I found a song Caroline had not sung in her church:
"His Name is Wonderful" by Audrey Mae Mieir.
I began teaching it to her,
It was one of my favorites that I had learned as a teenager.

"His name is Wonderful, His name is Wonderful,
His name is Wonderful, Jesus, my Lord;
He is the mighty King, Master of everything.
His name is Wonderful, Jesus, my Lord.

He's the great Shepherd, the Rock of all ages,
Almighty God is He;
Bow down before Him, Love and adore Him,
His name is Wonderful, Jesus, my Lord."

Soon, Caroline was singing with me.
As we sang, my thoughts jumped back almost fifty years.
I could see myself, driving the car on the way to church,
And worshipping the Lord through this song.

My spirit leaped.
Fifty years ago, I never dreamed I'd be singing...
This song of worship...with my six year old granddaughter,
I was filled with awe and joy.

Five decades ago, I was dreaming of finishing high school.
I was looking forward to college.
I dreamed of someday being married.
But even those short sighted desires seemed so far away from completion.

But was I dreaming of holding a sweet granddaughter on my lap?
Was I dreaming of worshipping the Lord with our Caroline?
I couldn't even fathom such a dream.

And now...here we are.
And I am taken back!!
And I am brought to the realization of God's all- knowing love for me.

Decades ago, I gave my heart to the Lord.
"Whatever You want, Lord. Wherever You want, Lord.
I dedicate my life to You."

Yes...I had some dreams and desires.
But I asked the Lord to make my desires those *HE* had for me.

Psalm 37:4 says,
"Delight yourself in the Lord;
And He will give you the desires of your heart."

It is amazing to me that God knew my heart better than I did.
He knew my deepest desires...those I could not see.
He knew me because He is the God who created me.
And He loves me.

God made my dreams come true!!
What dreams?
The dreams I never had...but He knew my heart.

Thank you, Lord, for fulfilling this dream I never knew I had.
Thank you, Lord, for the blessing of singing a worship song I loved long ago.
Thank you for the awe that comes with singing that song with Caroline!
Thank you!! You are so good!
Your Name truly is wonderful!

"ISN'T HE AMAZING?"

My mother found great pleasure in doing crafts.
When I was newly married, she found joy in helping me decorate.
Her ceramic creations lined shelves and adorned walls.
The manger scene she meticulously painted is one of my "treasures".
Afghans were knitted for children and grandchildren.
I still feel a sense of joy and awe when I show Mom's creations to friends.
"Look at this beautiful manger scene My Mom gave to me.
Isn't it amazing?
My Mom made it with her own hands!"

I love to go on "photo shoots" during autumn.
I choose a time when I can travel over the nearby mountain.
I stop at different sites along the river.
It is a time of stillness and serenity...
A time to enjoy God's beautiful creation...
A time of peace.

Psalm 19:1 says,
*"The heavens are telling of the glory of God;
And their expanse is declaring the work of His hands."*

Think about these words from the old hymn,
"This Is My Father's World", by Maltbie Babcock:

*"This is my Father's world,
And to my listening ears
All nature sings
And round me rings
The music of the spheres.*

This is my Father's world:
I rest me in the thought
Of rocks and trees,
Of skies and seas—
His hands the wonders wrought.

This is my Father's world,
Oh let me ne'er forget
That though the wrong seems oft so strong,
God is the ruler yet."

Yes! The creator of the world is my Father.
He is the "Heavenly Daddy" of all who believe in His Son, Jesus.
Father, Son, and Holy Spirit all had a part in Creation.

I know that my Mom's creativity was a gift from the Creator.
She made beautiful objects out of ordinary materials.
HE made the heavens and the earth out of *NOTHING!*
HE spoke...and it happened.
At the same time, *HE* placed within *HIS* Creation a gift...
The gift of seed to reproduce after its own kind.
All of nature has descended from that original command.
The breath of God was the source of all that is.

When I look at Creation...
I want to share it with others.
I am thankful He has given it to me to enjoy.
He has decorated my world with majesty.
His creation lines the rivers and adorns the skies.
He has meticulously painted the rich colors of autumn.
He has knitted this world together...and holds it there.
I breathe in the beauty.
I treasure it.
With a deep sense of joy and awe, I say to you...
"Look at this beautiful world my Father gave to me.
Isn't it amazing?
My Heavenly Father made it with His own hands.
Isn't *HE* amazing?"

CHRISTMAS KEEPSAKES

TO MELT

THE DEVOTED HEART

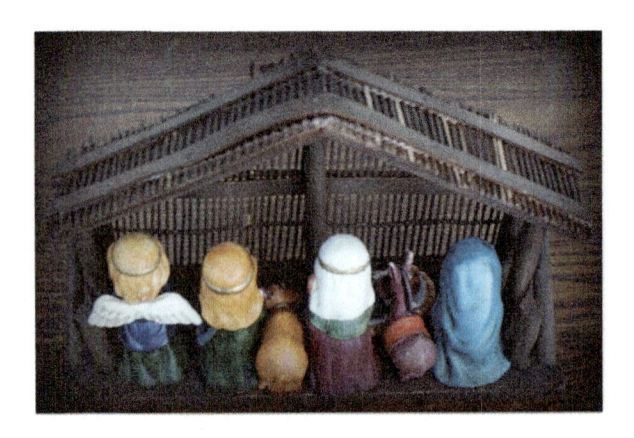

"CLOSER"

My four year old granddaughter, Caroline, helped me decorate this year.
She carefully unwrapped and set up the "kids' manger scene".
It is a "kid- proof" crèche which the grandkids enjoy!

I paid no attention to her diligent work, until she was finished.
I glanced at it and noticed that it looked different than if I had set it up.
I almost bent down to rearrange it, when I stopped!
It was almost as if the Lord was saying..."This is as it should be."

Caroline had placed each figure of the scene shoulder to shoulder.
Mary, Joseph, the shepherd, the angel, the animals…
They were all looking at the baby Jesus.
They were all as close to Jesus as they could be.

No one was looking at each other.
No one in the scene was faced outward.
I could see no faces, because every eye was gazing on the Savior!

We sing, "Oh, Come Let us Adore Him".
Do we really come and adore Him?
Or do we just look from a distance?
Or, perhaps, we don't look at all.

Caroline had the right idea!
How close can I get to Jesus?

This Christmas, let us *REALLY* come to Him!
REALLY LOOK at HIM!
HE is the Son of God.
HE lived, and *HE* died, for you!
Open your heart to Him.
Receive Him as your Savior.

Luke 2:11 says,
"For today in the city of David,
There has been born FOR YOU
A Savior, who is Christ the Lord."

"CHRISTMAS KEEPSAKES"

Being a mother is one of God's greatest gifts.
I loved being Mommy to four "exceptional" daughters.
When they were little, I especially enjoyed Christmas time.
We had special books we would read and special songs we would sing.
I found great joy in teaching them the true meaning of Christmas!
The wonder of the coming of Jesus, as a tiny baby, filled our lives.

The above picture is an image of our daughter, Sarah, with her baby boy, "CJ"!
As I took the photo, her eyes were on her baby.
He was the center of her attention.
He is her precious gift from God.
He is her "treasure".

I sometimes wonder what it must have been like to be Mary, the mother of Jesus.
I know she was young, possibly only fifteen!
But, she was an exceptional woman of God.
She was a woman who knew God's Word.
We see that truth in Luke 1.
Her praise to her Lord includes many references to Old Testament teachings.
And God chose her for the amazing task of being the mother of His Son!

I find one of the most insightful glimpses into Mary's soul in one Bible verse.
The setting is shortly after she had given birth.
She and her Child are in a stable.
She is using a manger for her Baby's crib.
She and Joseph and the Child had just received a visit from the shepherds.
The shepherds had found them in this unlikely place because angels had appeared.

The angels had told them,
*"...Today in the city of David there has been born for you a Savior, who is Christ the Lord.
This will be a sign for you: you will find a baby wrapped in cloths and lying in a manger."*
(Luke 2:11, 12)

What was Mary's response to all this "excitement"?
"But Mary treasured all these things, pondering them in her heart." (Verse 19)
Mary focused in on the wonder of it all…She thought about this treasure.
She was not bothered by the stable sights or the animal sounds.
She was not complaining about the barnyard smells or the inconveniences.
She was not focused on the fact that her surroundings were not perfect or ideal.
She saw the Treasure.

This Christmas…I wish for you…and for me…
A focus on the treasure.
A "keeping" of the important…
A "pondering" of the precious and the priceless.

I wish for you peaceful moments…
Moments away from the hurrying…
Moments away from trying to make everything "perfect", as we Moms tend to do.
Moments to look into the eyes of your children and grandchildren and see the wonder.
Moments to look into their hearts.
Moments to share.
Moments to keep…and treasure…and ponder.

I wish for you quiet moments…
Moments of focusing on what is really important this Christmas season.
Moments to read the Christmas story from the Bible…for yourself…all alone.
Moments to ponder the angel's words…
*"I bring you good news of great joy which will be for all the people…
…There has been born FOR YOU a Savior, who is Christ the Lord."* (Verses 10 and 11)

Christmas will come…and Christmas will go.
The Christmas treats will have been devoured.
The gifts will have been unwrapped.
The decorations will be put away.
The excitement will dwindle.
All of these temporary things…you cannot keep.

There are many things about Christmas you CAN keep, however.
Ponder the priceless…the eternal…
Let these truths be your "Christmas Keepsakes".
Keep them in your heart!

"MAGNIFICENCE DRESSED IN AN APRON"

Early morning text from my daughter, Sarah:
"Caroline is all dressed up and bringing an apron in case you want to make something.
Not sure where she got the idea she was going to your house today,
But are you free at all for a couple hours?"

Thankfully, Grandma was free.
When I opened the door, I was greeted by the "magnificence" of a "Princess"!
Caroline was adorned in a beautiful white chiffon dress.
In her hand, she carried a simple cotton apron.

When we arrived at Grandma's house,
Caroline asked me to tie the apron on her.
I lifted her up to the counter's baking section.
Caroline's day was spent serving Grandma's needs…
A teaspoon of this…a cup of that…
Whatever I needed, Caroline provided!

On that day, my Caroline reminded me of Jesus.
HE is the very definition of "magnificence"!
Yet, *HE* came to earth, "dressed in an apron".

HE was a king, but *HE* came as a baby.
HE left His throne, and was laid in a manger.
He closed His eyes to the glory of Heaven,
And opened them to the simplicity of a stable.

Philippians 2: 5-8 reveal the humility of the King.
"Have this attitude in yourselves which was also in Christ Jesus,

Who, although He existed in the form of God,
Did not regard equality with God a thing to be grasped,
But emptied Himself, taking the form of a bond-servant,
And being made in the likeness of men.
Being found in appearance as a man, He humbled Himself
By becoming obedient to the point of death, even death on a cross."

Jesus Christ took on servant hood!
HE became a servant!
And He asks us to have the same attitude.
He asks us to seek, not to *BE* served, but to serve!

My Grandma used to have a plaque on her wall that read:

"Jesus first
Others next
Yourself last"

Perhaps, much of the *JOY* of the Christmas season,
Is found in that simple truth!

So, dear friends,
In all the festivities of the Christmas season,
In all the magnificence,
Let us not forget our aprons!

"CHRISTMAS...REMEMBERING THE MOMENTS"

Decorating the Christmas tree...
Baking the Christmas Cookies...
Shopping for the perfect presents...
Wrapping the perfect presents...
Placing the perfect presents under the tree...
Delivering the perfect presents...
Christmas Caroling...
Christmas Concerts...
Christmas Pageants...
Entertaining Guests...
Visiting relatives...
Exhaustion!

A few weeks ago I asked my four daughters a question.
They are all grown now....
Three of them married with children of their own.
The question?
What is your favorite childhood Christmas memory?
I told them it could be a gift or a tradition or something we did or...
Anything.

Before I give you their answers...
I need to tell you something.
When our children were growing up...
Christmas was a very special time for us...for me...
I loved reading them books about Christmas.
I loved teaching them about the birth of Jesus.

I loved singing Christmas songs with them.
I loved shopping for the "perfect presents".
I made sure each child received the same number of gifts...
(Sometimes, I even wrapped batteries...ha-ha.)
I wanted them to love the presents they unwrapped.
I wanted them to be excited!
I went to great lengths to make sure they were happy!
And...They were!!

Now...I will give you their answers:
What is their favorite Christmas memory?

Tabitha...
"...Baking Christmas cookies with her grandmas and aunts,
After which she would pretend she was asleep,
So she could get carried to "Gram Gram"
And cuddle in her arms."

Rebecca...
"Going to a store and seeing a touch lamp that she really wanted,
But we had been unable to find,
And Daddy got it for her."
And also "getting up Christmas morning, and Daddy,
Who never made breakfast for them,
Made hot chocolate and English muffins."

Sarah...
"Decorating and putting up the manger scene...
After the tree was decorated, we would turn off all the lights,
Except the tree lights, and sit in the dark and look at the tree."
And also...the following memory she shares with Bethany...

Bethany...
"The year we opened all our Christmas presents and then...
Dad said, "Let's go to New York City!"
So we got ready, drove to New York City,
Spent the day there together, and drove home."

Now...in that list of favorite memories...
Do any of you see anything about all that work Mom did...
Finding and wrapping those perfect presents??
Nope...not there!!!!!

It is not that they did not appreciate and enjoy those gifts...
I know they did!
It is that they appreciated the most...
The *TIME* we spent together...
The things we *DID* together...
The spontaneity and caring and fun and family.

You never know when a moment will become a memory!
I have many favorite Christmas memories.
One of the memories etched into my mind??
Christmas 1963.
I had accepted Christ that fall.
One night, after everyone else had retired for the evening...
I lay on the couch and just gazed at the Christmas tree.
It held new meaning for me that year.
Christmas had a richness I had not before experienced.
As I looked at the tree, I thought of the true meaning of Christmas.
I considered the eternal life represented by the evergreen tree.
The evergreen does not lose its needles every fall.
It stands the same ...always green.

As I considered the wonder of the Christmas story...
I remained in awe of what Jesus had done...
Being born...knowing He would die for my sin...
Giving me eternal life.
What a Wonderful Savior!

What can I give back to God this Christmas?
What does He ask of me?
The same thing He asks of His children every other day.
1 John 3:23 says...
"This is His commandment,
That we believe in the name of His Son Jesus Christ,
And love one another, just as He commanded us."

Whatever we do this Christmas...
We should, above all else, be sure we have placed our trust in Christ.
We should then demonstrate our faith in the Lord Jesus.
We should show our love for each other.

Memories are valuable.
They often teach us what was...and is...important in life.
So...try not to stress too much if you cannot find the "perfect present".
It may not be quite as important as your child thinks it is right now.
Years from now...what will be their favorite memories?
Moments held in their hearts...
Gifts of your time...and demonstrations of your love.

And remember to spend time with Jesus.
After all...it is *HIS* birthday.
Sit down in front of the Christmas tree...
Think of the significance of eternity.
Think about what He did as a demonstration of *HIS* love.
Spend time in His presence.
Put your trust in *HIM*!
Give Him your heart!

"Where are YOU??"

The manger scene...
"The reason for the season"...
The true meaning of Christmas...
The backdrop for "The Greatest Story"!

Many "manger scenes" have been created over the years...
My Mom worked hours and hours on the one pictured above.
It is truly a beautiful creation!

Have you ever seen yourself in this scene?
No, not physically, perhaps!
But try looking "between the lines".

The Bible, in John 3:16, says...
"For GOD so loved THE WORLD, that He gave HIS ONLY BEGOTTEN SON...".
Do you see where you are in this whole scenario?
You are the reason for it!

Have you ever heard anyone make this statement to a loved one...?
"No one will ever come between us!"
Well...look carefully at John 3:16, quoted above.
Who came between *GOD* and *HIS ONLY SON*?
YOU and *I* did!

The birth of the Christ child was planned...from eternity past.
God knew every detail.
And He did it for you!
You were the reason!

The Father and the Son knew Jesus would be born...
A tiny baby in a humble manger bed.
The Father and the Son knew Jesus would live a perfect life.
The Father and the Son knew Jesus would die...
The perfect sacrifice for my sin...and yours.
The Father and the Son knew Jesus would rise again.